20

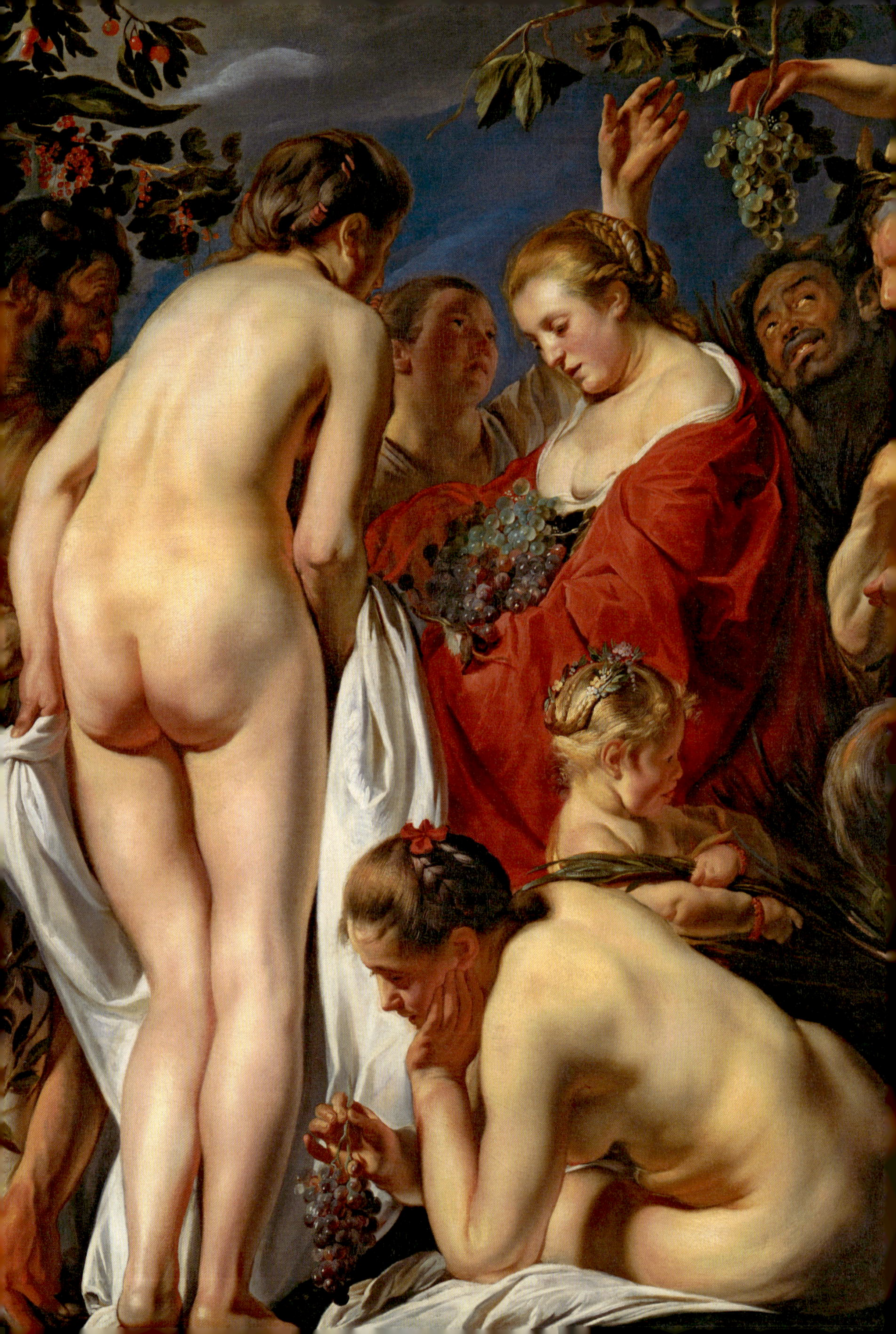

Jacques Jordaens

(1593–1678)

Allegories of Fruitfulness and Abundance

SilvanaEditoriale

Royal Museums
of Fine Arts of Belgium

Contents

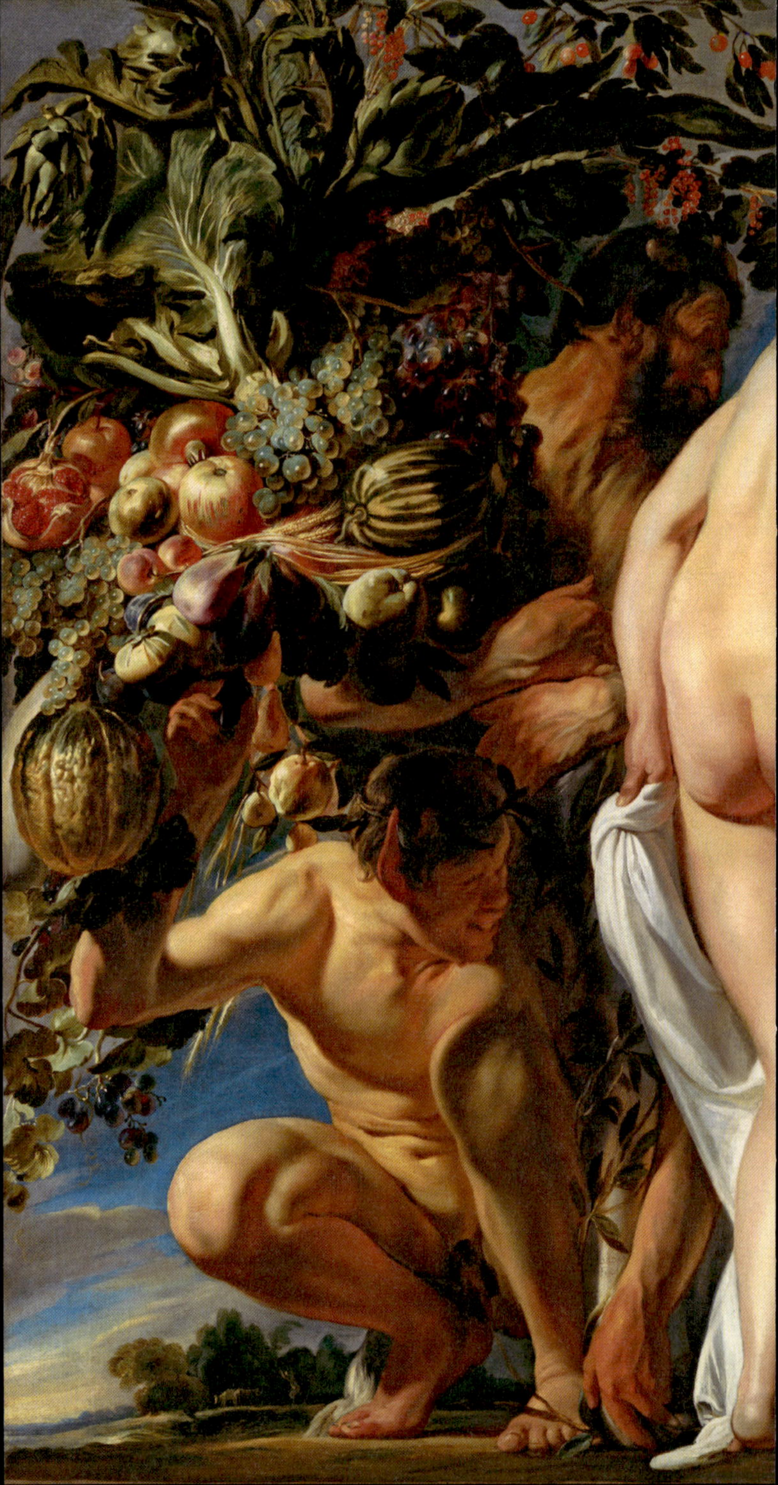

Jacques Jordaens,
Allegory of Fertility,
ca. 1623–25, Brussels,
RMFAB, oil on canvas,
180 × 241 cm, inv. 119

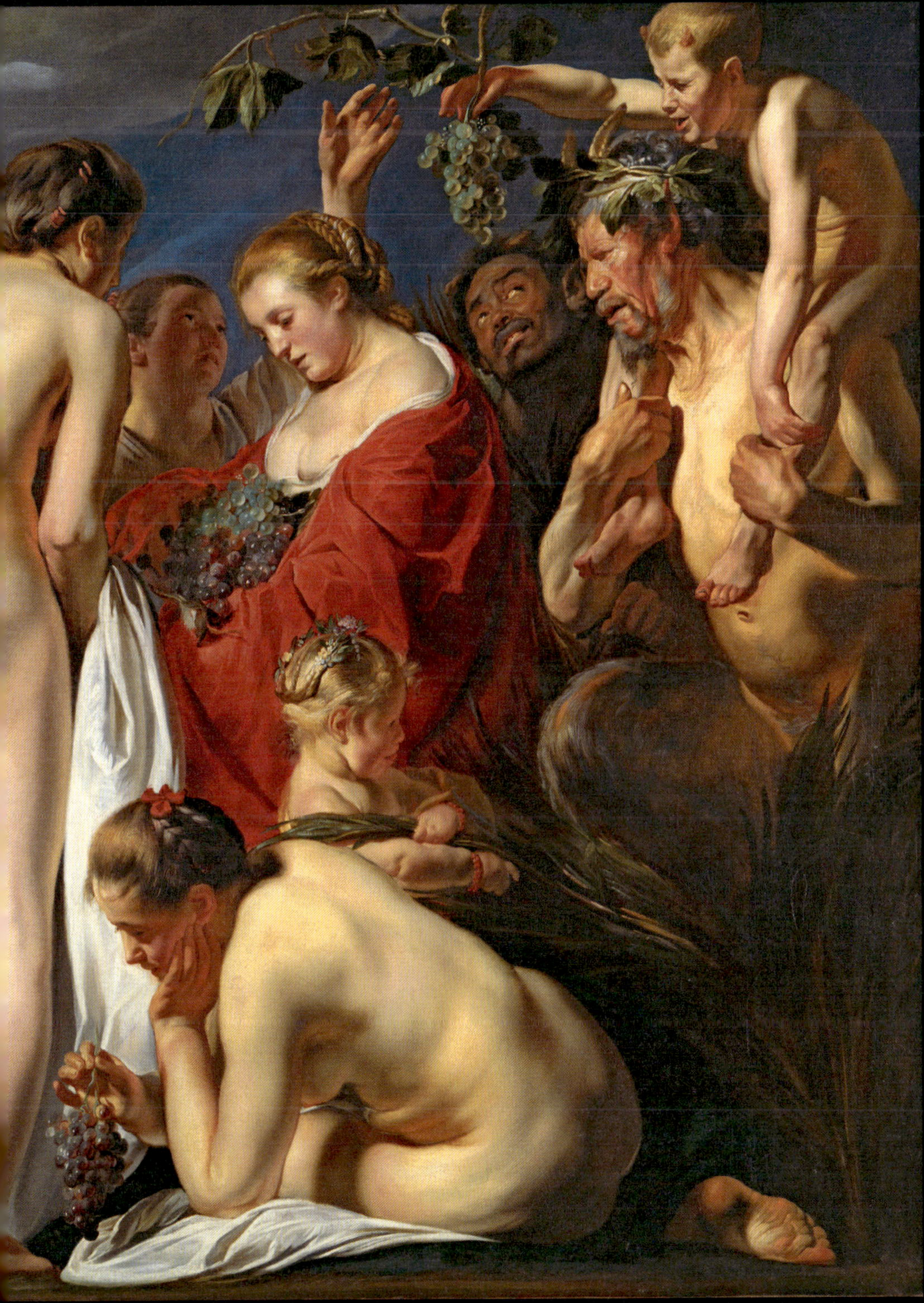

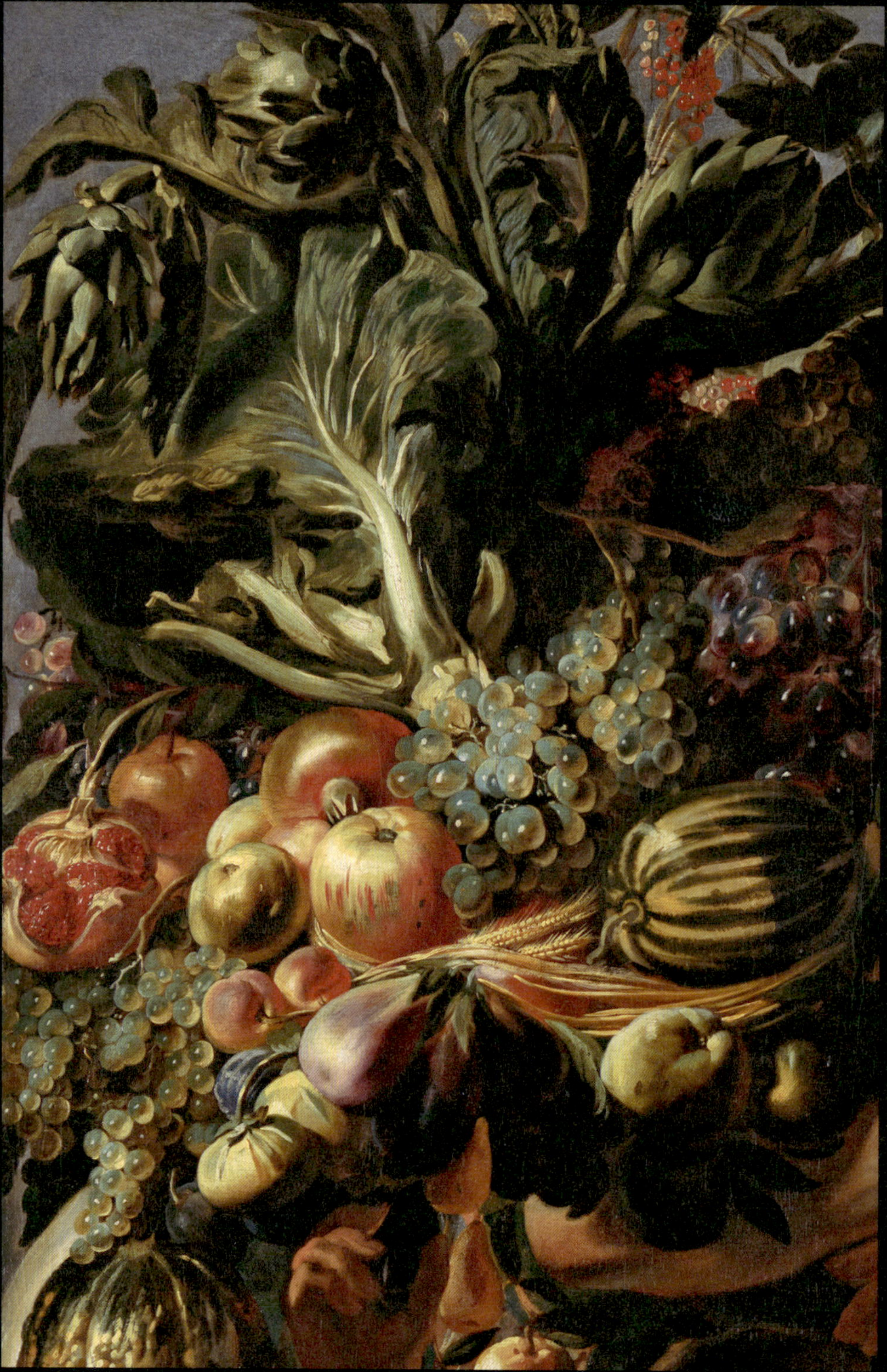

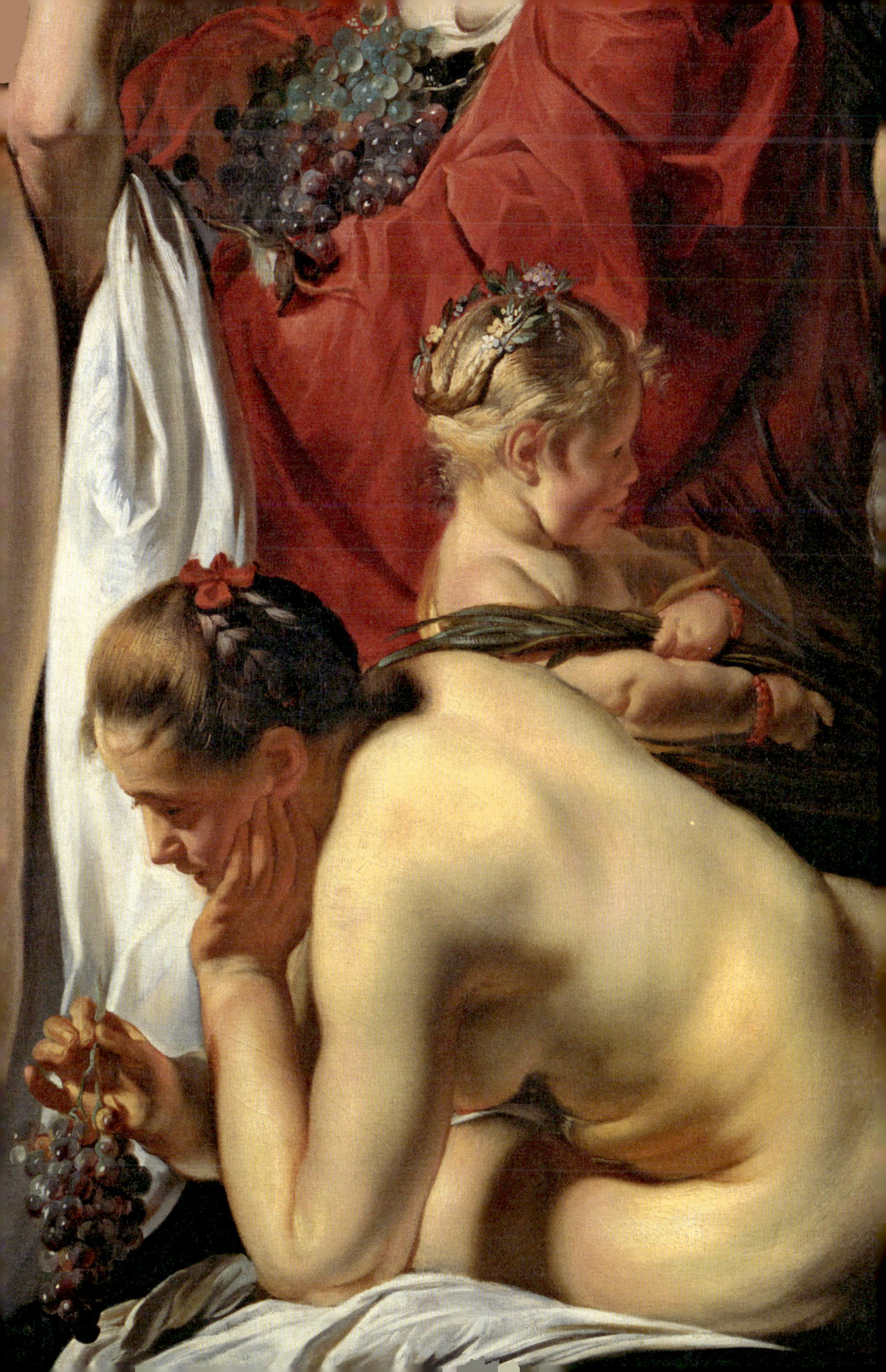

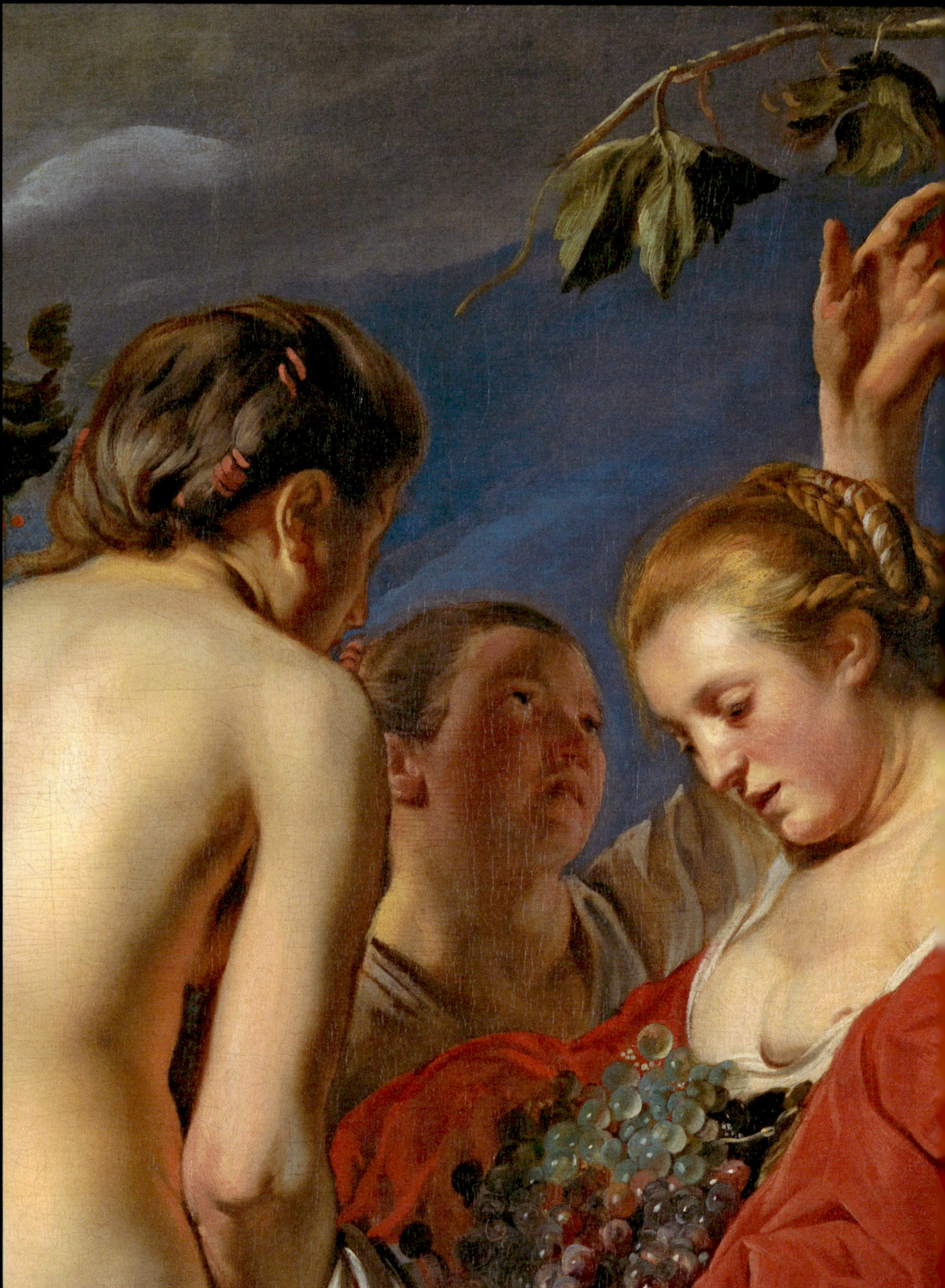

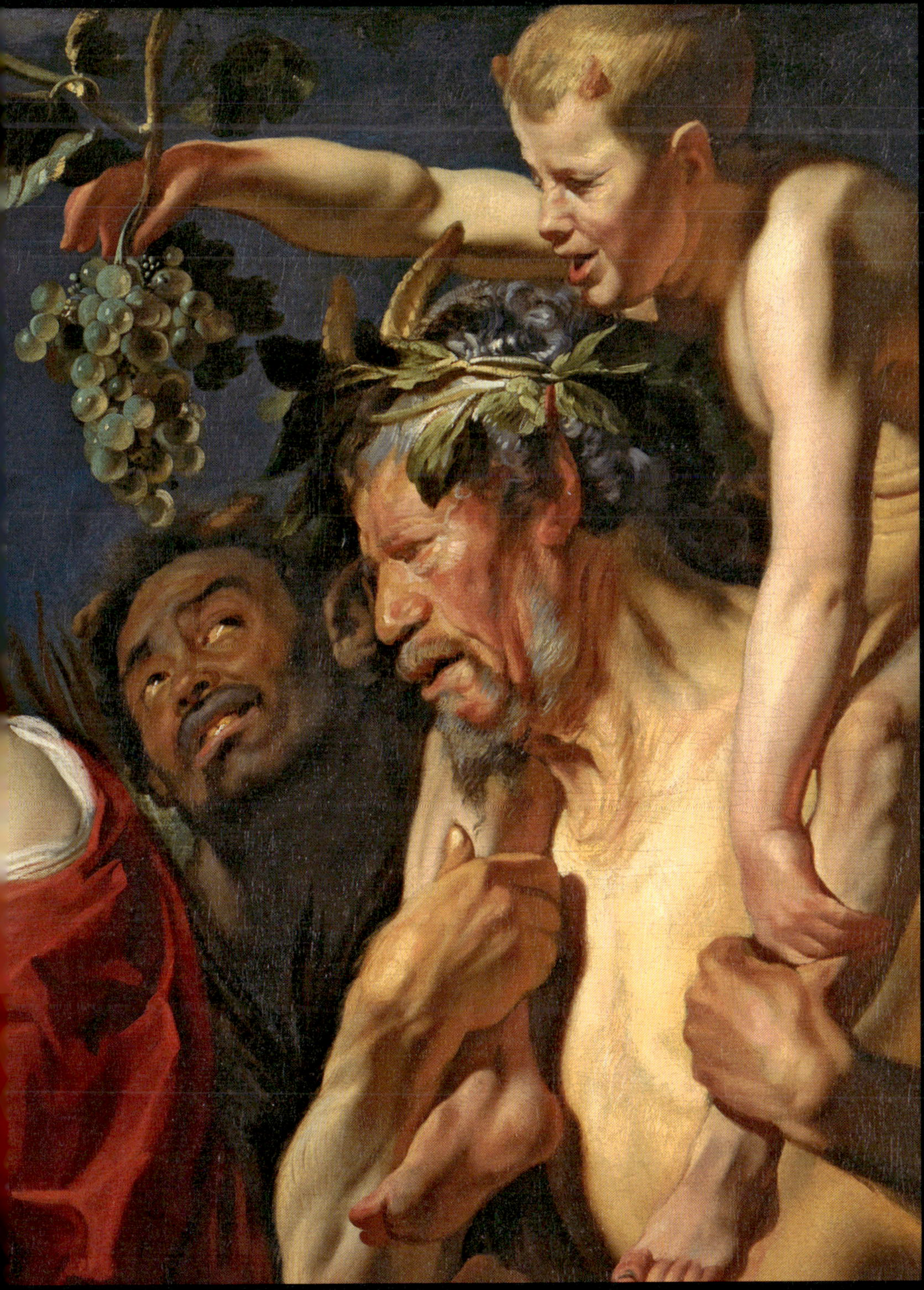

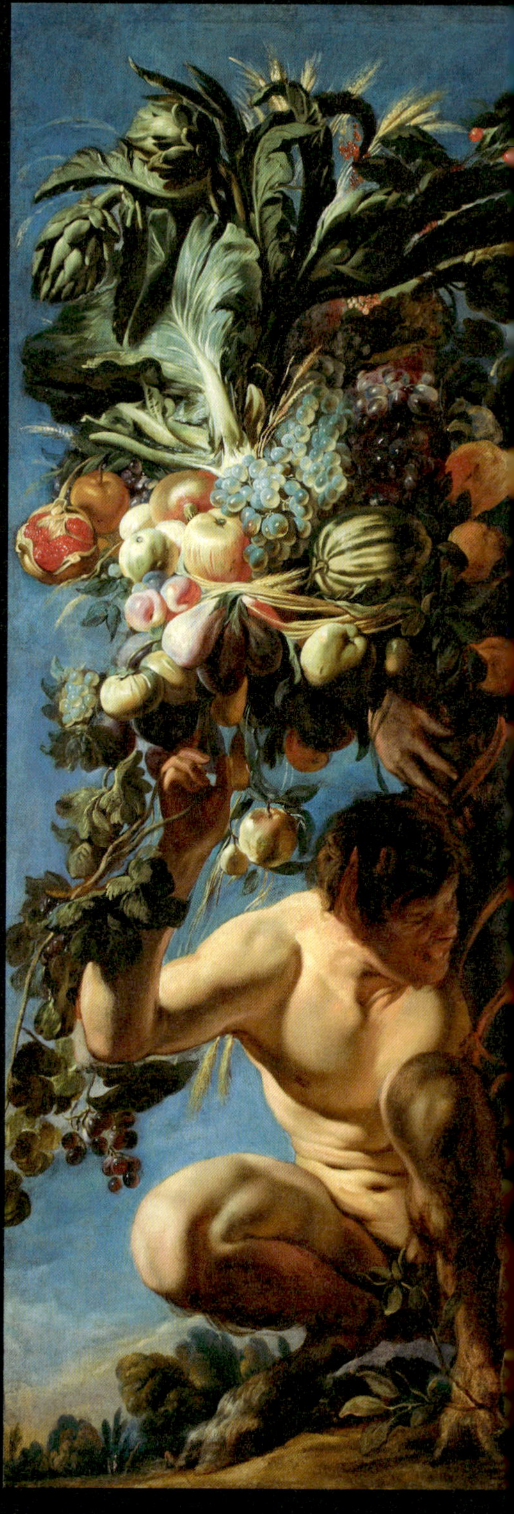

Jacques Jordaens,
Allegory of Fruitfulness,
ca. 1623–25, with later additions, ca. 1640?,
London, The Wallace Collection, oil on canvas,
201.1 × 229.5 cm,
inv. P120

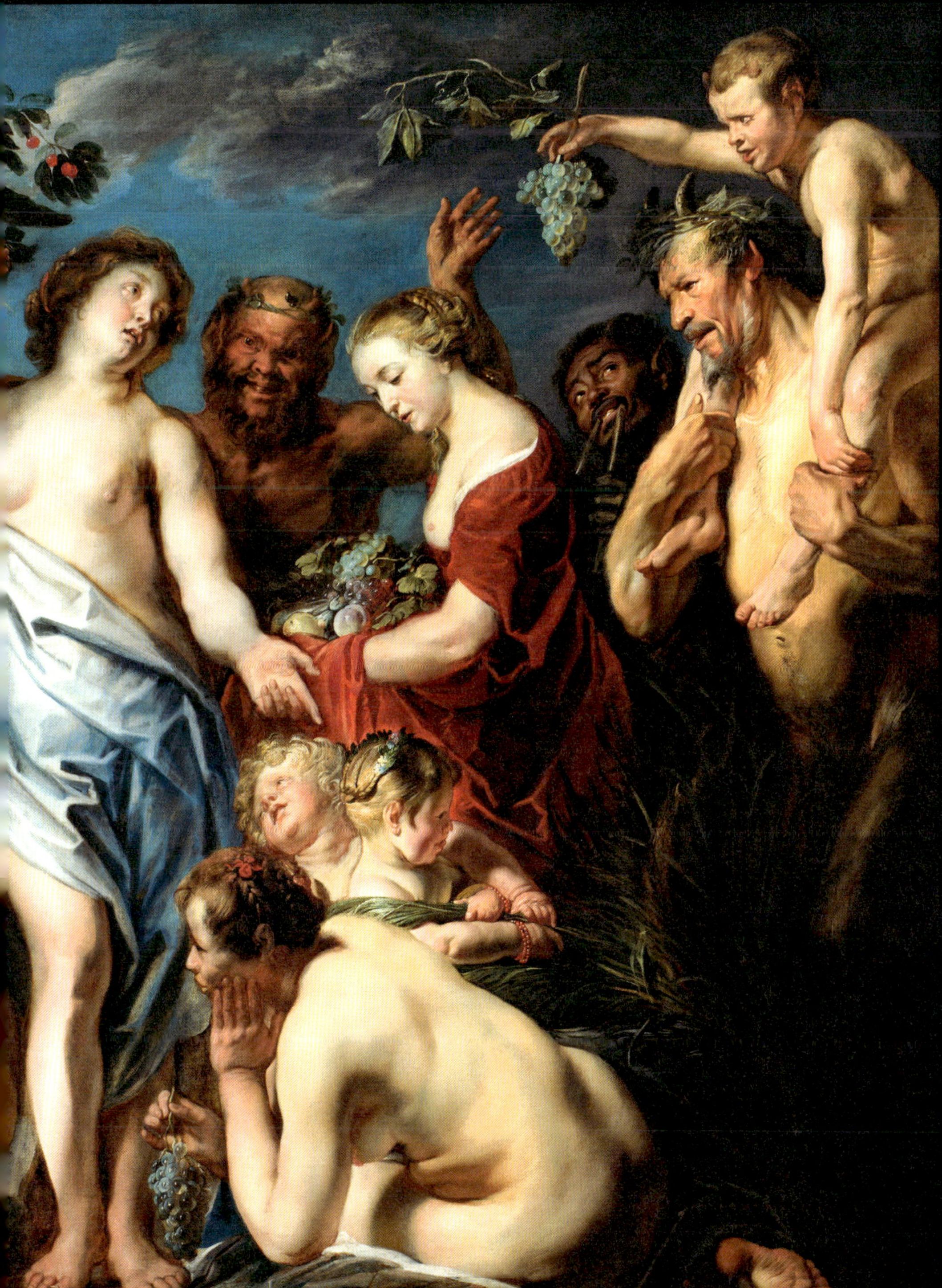

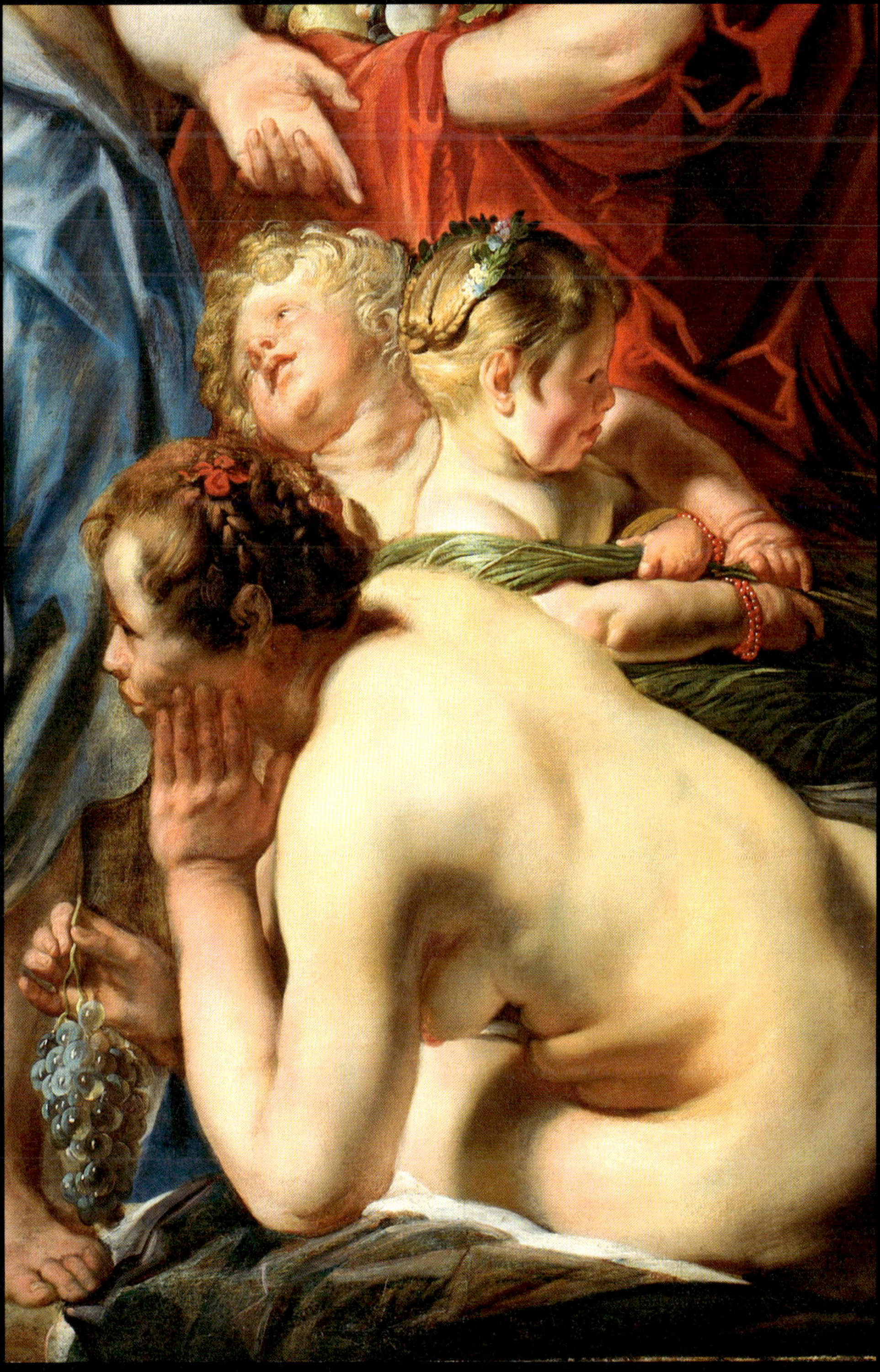

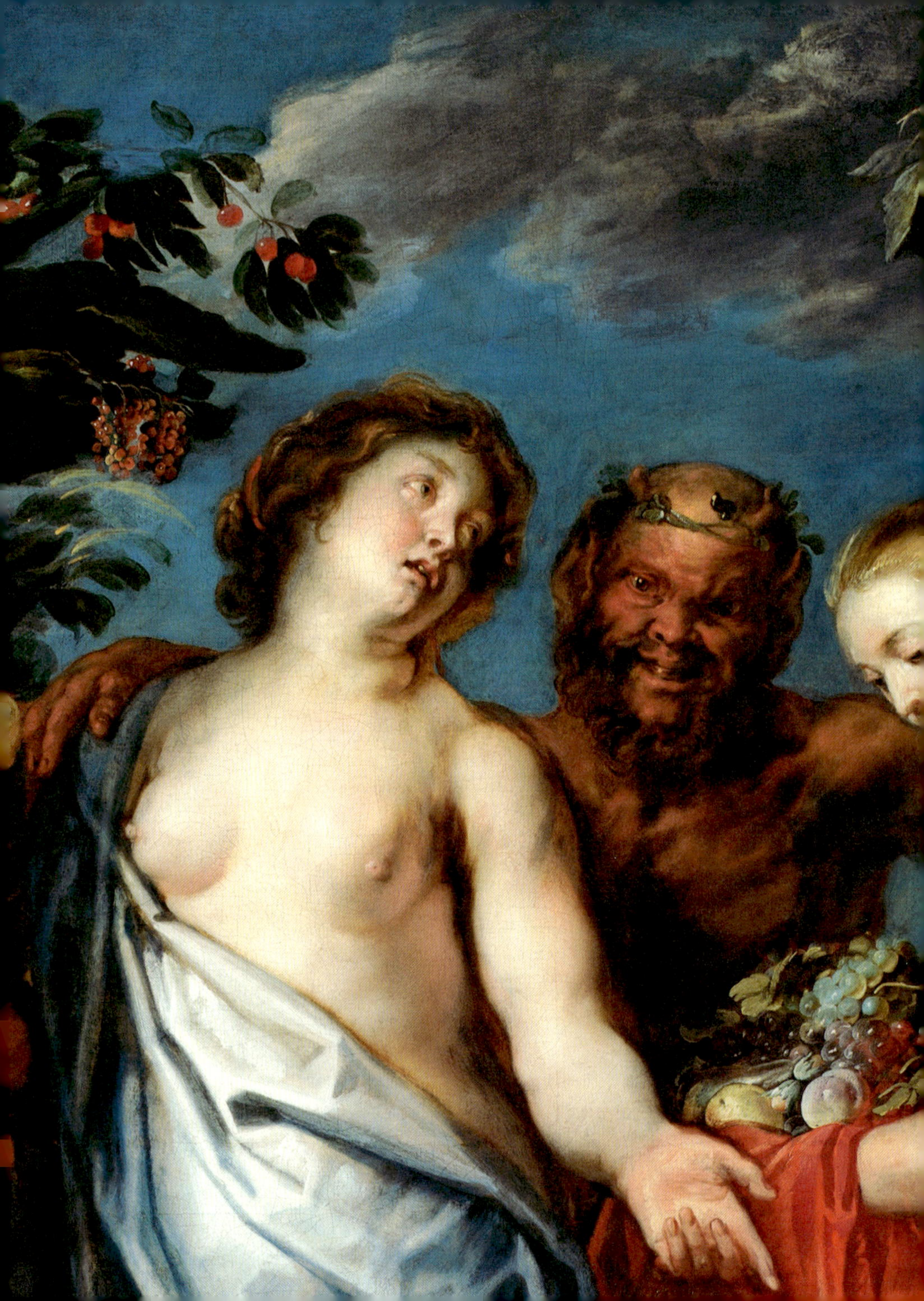

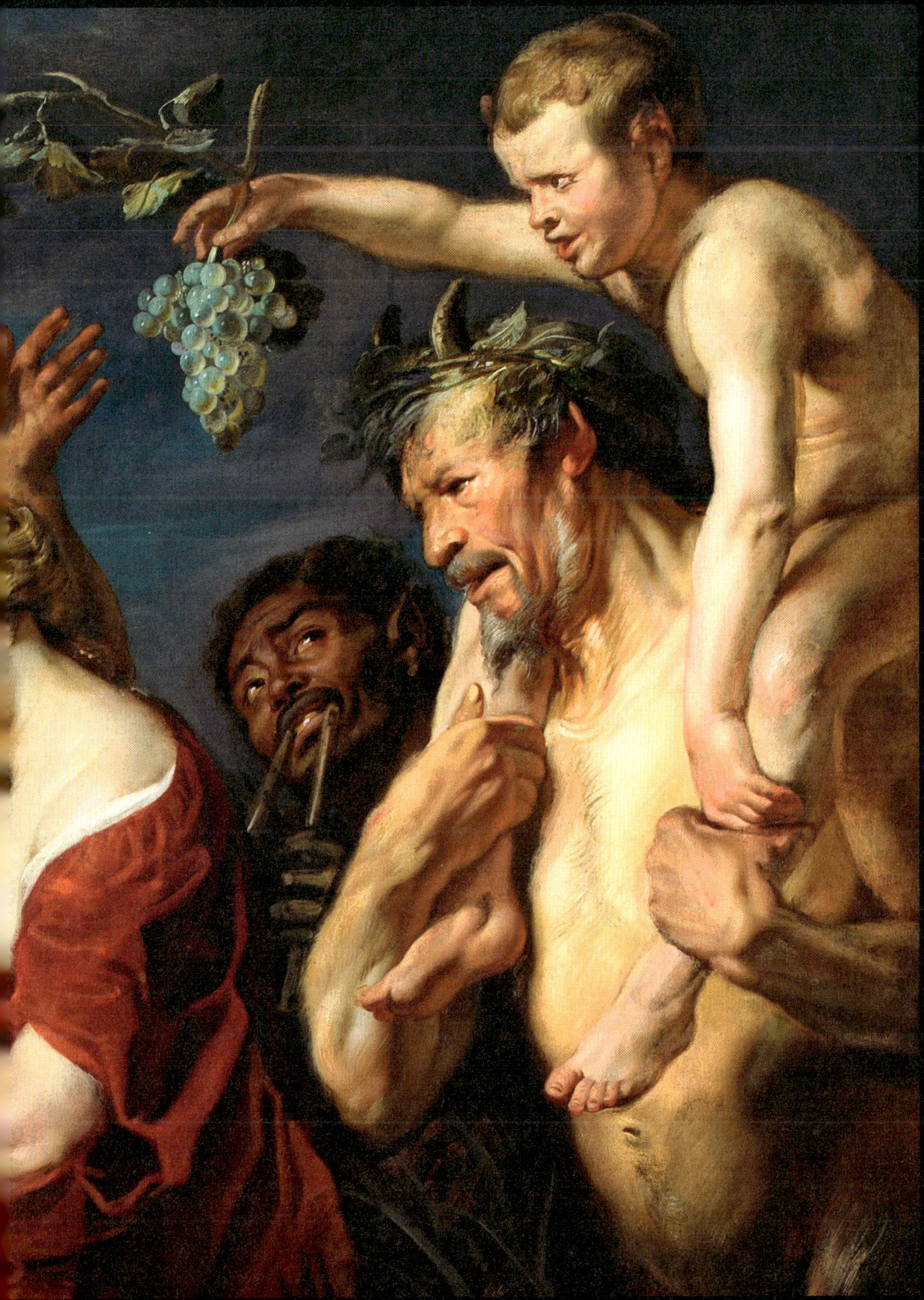

I. Art Historical Analysis

The Fullness of Things: Jordaens Celebrates Nature's Bounty

IRENE SCHAUDIES

"O most radiant lights of the firmament, that guide through heaven the gliding year, O Liber and bounteous Ceres, if by your grace Earth changed Chaonia's acorn for the rich corn ear, and blended draughts of Achelous with the newfound grapes, and you Fauns, the rustics' ever present gods (come trip it, Fauns, and Dryad maids withal!) 'tis of your bounties I sing."[1] So proclaims Virgil at the outset of the *Georgics,* and the list of players and props – Bacchus and Ceres, grain and grapes, satyrs and nymphs and rustic folk – could just as well describe any of Jordaens's numerous paintings of Nature's abundance. For narrative interest he seems to have fleshed out these flourishing scenes with references to Ovid's *Metamorphoses,* in particular the story of how the horn of plenty – or Cornucopia – was created. In Ovid's version of this well-known myth, Hercules engages in a heated contest for the hand of the lovely Deianeira with the shape-shifting river god Achelous. The latter transforms himself repeatedly during the pitched battle, entering combat as a human being and then becoming first a snake, then a bull. The mighty Hercules, unshaken, eventually puts an end to the conflict by tearing off one of Achelous's horns while the river god has assumed the form of a bull. The naiads – as water nymphs, his notional daughters – take this trophy and fill it with fruit and flowers, thereby sanctifying it, and present it as an offering to the goddess of Plenty (Bona Copia). This gesture, in Achelous's telling, seems to ease the discomfort and shame of his defeat.[2] Perhaps not by chance, Achelous figures in both text sources – Virgil and Ovid – for in antiquity the river god was often venerated for his symbolic role as bringer of water and hence fruitfulness. The stunning visualization of these beloved passages from antiquity would no doubt have appealed to Jordaens's patrons, who seem to have been drawn largely from Antwerp's wealthy and well-educated merchant community.

Though it is impossible to say precisely which edition(s) of Ovid Jordaens consulted, his earliest *Allegory of Fertility* – known as the *Homage to Pomona* (fig. 1)[3] – points in the direction of Karel van Mander's *Wtlegghingh op den Metamorphosis,* an interpretive and often

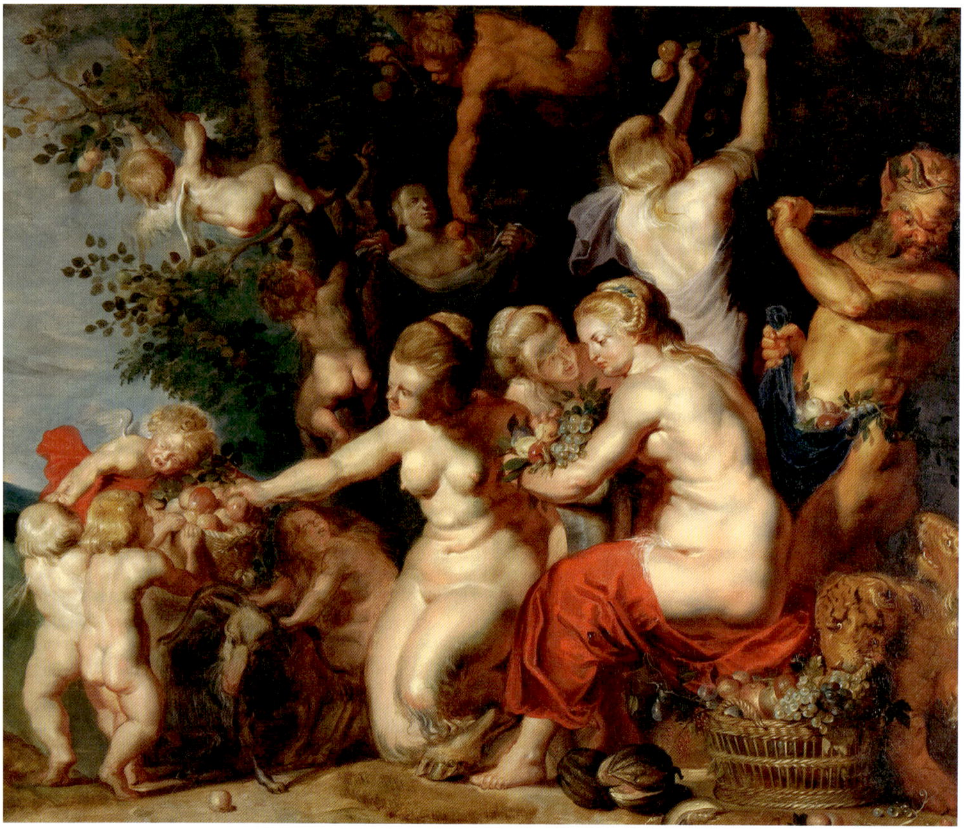

1. Jacques Jordaens, *Homage to Pomona,* ca. 1615, Miami Beach, Florida, Bass Museum of Art, oil on panel, 64 × 76 cm, inv. 79.275

moralizing guide to Ovid's collection of myths that was published as a supplement to *Het Schilder-boeck* in 1604.[4] Its overall composition was probably borrowed from Rubens's cabinet-sized Bacchanal of ca. 1613–14, now in the Pushkin Museum in Moscow (fig. 2).[5]

The seated nymph in the center of Jordaens's composition holds a cornucopia and is traditionally identified as Pomona, Roman goddess of gardening and "tree fruit," on account of the many apples being offered to her. Yet certain elements of the composition cast doubt on her presumed identity. Pomona is usually depicted as a chaste wood nymph who is eventually wooed with success by the shape-shifting god Vertumnus – indeed Jordaens even painted her this way in a later work based on a sketch by Rubens, in which Vertumnus has assumed the guise of an elderly woman in order to win the girl's confidence (fig. 3).[6] In the Bass painting, however, the principal figure is a comely nymph, nearly nude. She is furthermore attended by a satyress and surrounded by additional nymphs, putti, satyrs, and a grape-hungry tiger – inveterate minions of Pan and Bacchus, who are associated with scenes of lust and abandon rather

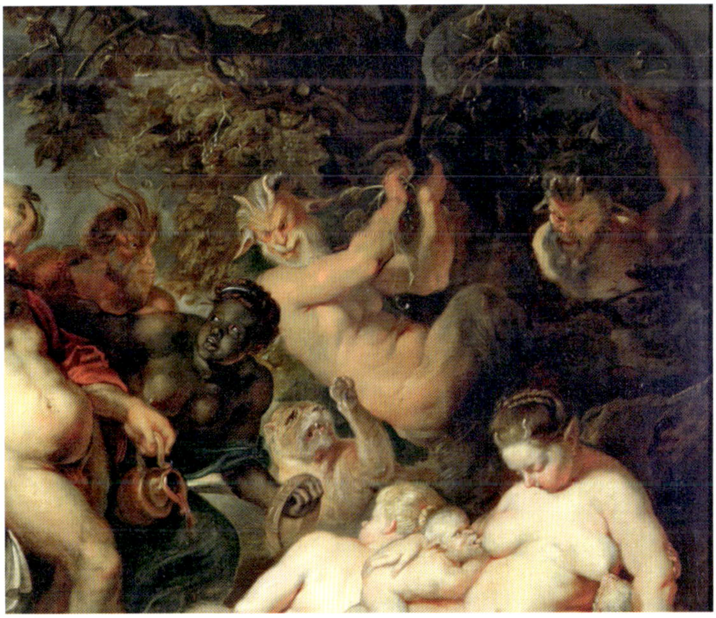

2. Peter Paul Rubens, *Bacchanal,* ca. 1613–14, Moscow, Pushkin State Museum of Fine Arts, oil on panel, 91 × 107 cm, inv. 2606

3. Jacques Jordaens after Peter Paul Rubens, *Vertumnus and Pomona,* 1638, Caramulo, Portugal, Museu do Caramulo, Fundação Abel e João de Lacerda, oil on canvas, 200 × 270 cm, inv. FAL 334

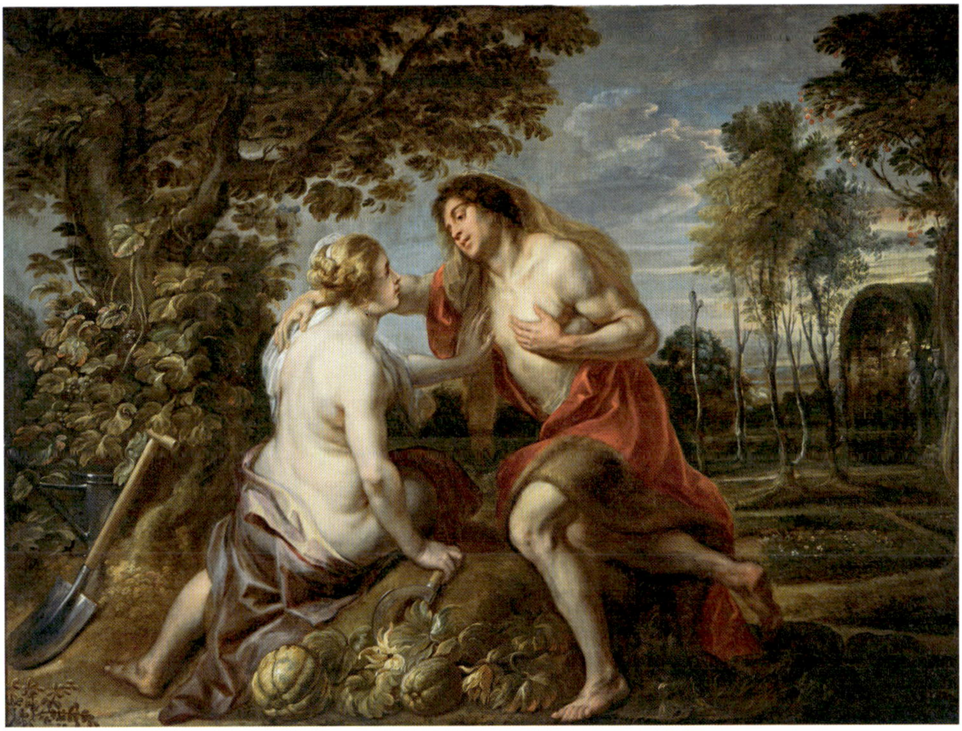

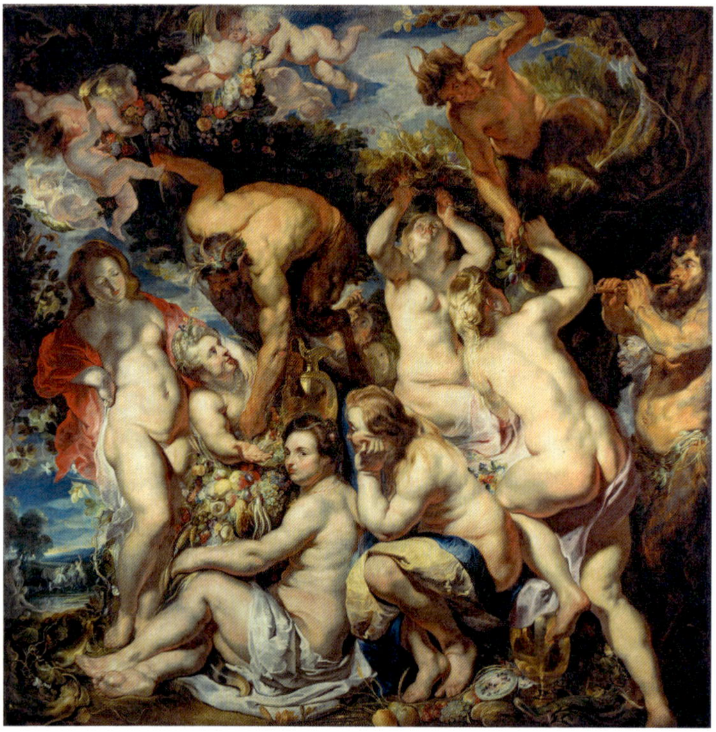

4. Jacques Jordaens, *Allegory of Fertility*, ca. 1616–17, Munich, Bayrische Staatsgemäldesammlungen, Alte Pinakothek, oil on canvas, 250 × 240 cm, inv. 10411

5. Peter Paul Rubens, *The Daughters of Cecrops Finding the Child Erichthonius*, ca. 1613–14, Vienna, Sammlung des Regierenden Fürsten von Liechtenstein, Vaduz, oil on canvas, 217.8 × 317.3 cm, inv. GE 111

than chastity. There is no body of water to evoke the role of the river god Achelous, nor do there seem to be any naiads in the vicinity, features that might seem to preclude the possibility that the scene represents the cornucopia myth. This apparent difficulty is resolved, however, by Van Mander's commentary in the *Wtlegghingh*.

In his discussion of the "hooren des Overvloeds," he also mentions Plutarch's version of the cornucopia myth, which refers to the horn being filled specifically with apples, the attribute of Pomona.[7]

The conflation of Pomona and Bona Copia has long dogged modern scholars of Jordaens, and the difficulty is compounded by the fact that Abundance as such – a personification conjured up by Renaissance humanists – can be associated with various ancient deities, including Ceres, Bacchus, Ops, Fortuna, Gaia, and a host of others, as long as they hold a cornucopia.[8] For Jordaens, such fine-grained scholarly distinctions may not have been important as long as at least one of these representatives of earth's fertility was notionally present – certainly since Van Mander's commentary, which was probably Jordaens's primary source on the subject, tends to leave the question open, mentioning each of these figures in turn in myths involving the abundance of nature.[9] Perhaps not coincidentally, Van Mander's extended discussion of the cornucopia mentions alternative versions of the myth in which Jupiter's mother gives the horn to Amalthea for the nourishment of her son – another favorite subject of Jordaens's.[10]

In a slightly later *Allegory of Fertility* from ca. 1616–17 (fig. 4),[11] which is far more ambitious

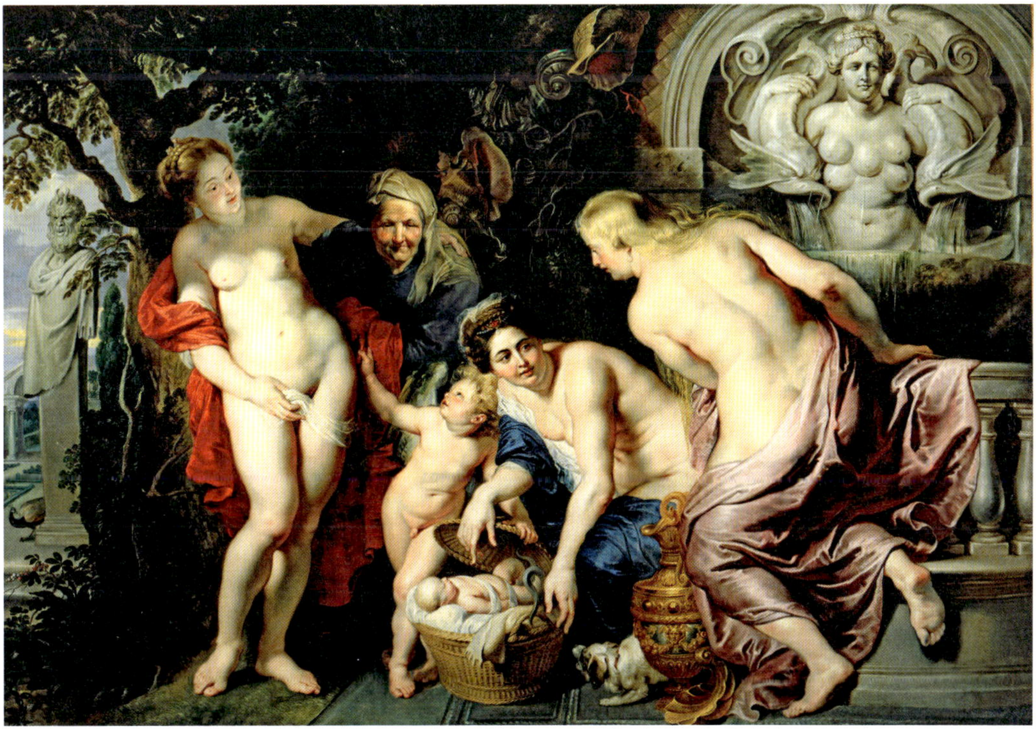

in scale than the cabinet-sized *Homage to Pomona,* Jordaens has adhered more closely to Ovid's text. The principal female figure is once again seated on the ground, nearly nude, and holding a lavish cornucopia. Together with the pearls and flowers that adorn her hair, this attribute identifies her as Bona Copia, the goddess of plenty who receives the first cornucopia in the *Metamorphoses.* Moreover, naiads bathe near the water's edge in the distance – a clear allusion to Achelous – and on the opposite bank a lusty satyr pursues a group of cows. As in the *Homage to Pomona,* Jordaens has drawn inspiration from Rubens. The standing nymph at the left of the *Allegory of Fertility,* for example, is directly inspired by the figure of Herse, youngest of three mythological sisters in Rubens's *Daughters of Cecrops Finding the Child Erichthonius* (fig. 5).[12] These two subjects may at first glance seem unrelated, but in fact the Cecrops myth highlights the fertility of the earth in a different way: according to Ovid, the snake-child Erichthonius is born of Gaia, the earth, after Vulcan spills his seed on her fertile ground in a futile attempt to rape the goddess Minerva. Rubens emphasized the notion of Gaia's fertility by placing the sisters before a fountain decorated with a half-length statue of Diana of Ephesus, the many-breasted goddess associated with Nature's fertility; in the background this idea is further underscored by a herm of Pan standing in the garden.[13] Jordaens has shifted these ideas into a conceptually simpler invention that deals directly with the notion of abundance rather than obliquely with Gaia, but he compensates the absence of Rubens's archeological rigor with lavish treatment and plenty of *copia*: colorful fruit and flowers scattered throughout;

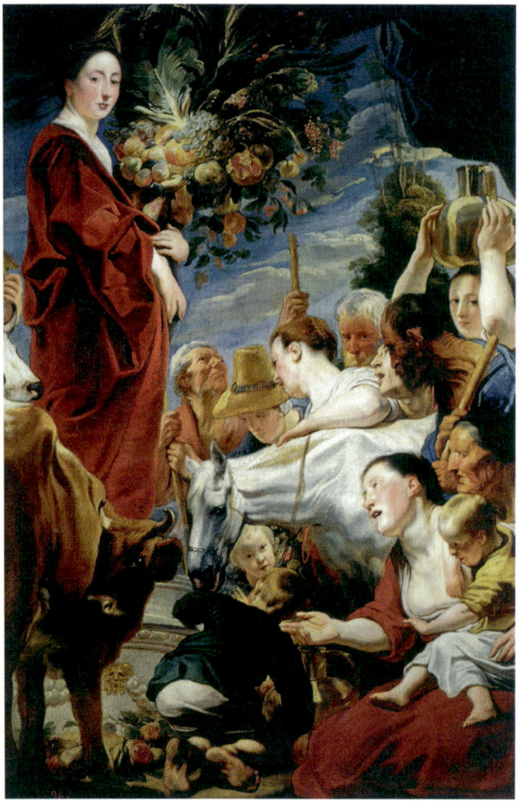

6. Jacques Jordaens, *Homage to Ceres,* ca. 1623–25 Madrid, Museo del Prado, oil on canvas, 165 × 112 cm, inv. PO15470

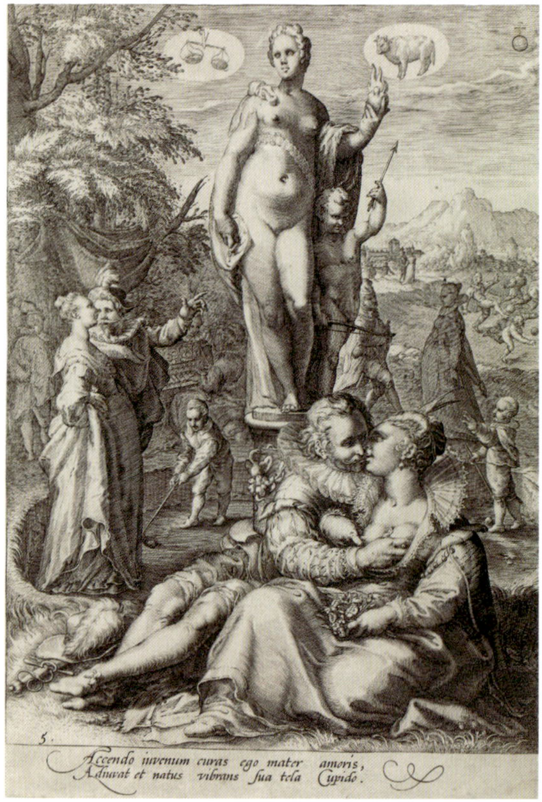

7. Jan Saenredam after Hendrick Goltzius, *Ceres,* 1596, London, British Museum, engraving, 450 × 323 mm, inv. 1850,1214.49

an abundance of pale, voluptuous nymphs; robust satyrs, browned by the sun; and swarms of putti adorning the trees with garlands. The ambitious monumentality of his figures also owes a considerable debt to the Antwerp painter Abraham Janssen, whose sculptural style was almost as important for his artistic development as Rubens's powerful fleshy nudes.

Jordaens's allegories of fertility and fruitfulness in Brussels and London – the subject of this study – evince a greater level of artistic and intellectual maturity than the works discussed above. In a much more direct way, they evoke the ancient world of Roman sarcophagi and sculpture in the round without sacrificing Jordaens's characteristic lifelike exuberance. The overall composition that is roughly shared by both paintings was inspired by a Roman sarcophagus of the 2nd century AD, which Jordaens could have known through a Renaissance engraving.

He may also – as Joost Vander Auwera will show in his contribution to this volume – have been familiar with drawings made directly from the (un)restored sarcophagus in Rome by one of his Antwerp colleagues. Rubens and Janssen are the most likely candidates, though no such drawing by either artist survives. Jordaens has filled this structural framework with figures based on no less than three statues also found in engraved compilations of famous antiquities that were widely circulated at the time. Perhaps not coincidentally, both works were painted – or at least initially conceived – in the mid-1620s, a period that saw Jordaens at his most archeologically engaged. This distinguishing feature may have been motivated in part by Jordaens's immediate artistic context. In 1619, Rubens acquired a splendid collection of antiquities from Sir Dudley Carleton, Charles I's envoy to the Low Countries, which he would eventually sell to the Duke of Buckingham in 1626. During the six years it was in Antwerp, its presence must have inspired artists like Jordaens to greater feats of appropriation, because at no other time in his career did he show so much interest in incorporating specific motifs from antique statuary into his inventions. His *Satyr and Peasant* of ca. 1619–20, for example, appends the head of the satyr Marsyas to the body of a Hellenistic fisherman in order to lend weight to his depiction of the satyr as a sort of natural philosopher, heir to Socrates and Silenus both.

Jordaens's *Homage to Ceres* (fig. 6), which likewise dates to ca. 1623–25, is less archeologically intense than the Brussels and London allegories, but relies more heavily on Virgil's *Georgics*.[14] Moreover, the very structure of the composition points strongly in the direction of a specific edition. Karel van Mander's Dutch translation of Virgil's famous poems, *Bucolica en Georgica, dat is, Ossen-stal en Landt-werk,* was published in 1597, and the woodcut decorating the introduction is based on Hendrik Goltzius's *Ceres* of 1596 (fig. 7).[15] With its innovative confrontation of a mythological personage and crowd of contemporary peasants, it almost certainly served as the source of visual inspiration for Jordaens's *Homage to Ceres.* Jordaens has aimed for a similar confrontation, perhaps even surpassing Goltzius in terms of the vivid fleshiness of both goddess and supplicants. The mantled goddess and especially her mingled peasant throng were probably also inspired by Caravaggio's *Madonna of the Rosary* of ca. 1606–07(fig. 8), who is similarly surrounded by a crowd of petitioners, some with dirty feet.[16]

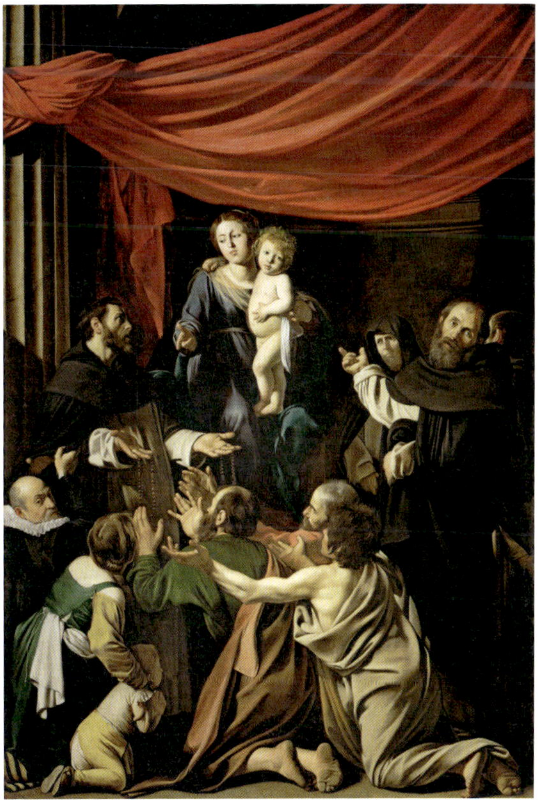

8. Caravaggio, *Madonna of the Rosary,* ca. 1606–07, Vienna, Gemäldegalerie, Kunsthistorisches Museum, oil on canvas, 364.5 × 249.5 cm, inv. GG_147

Individuals in Jordaens's crowd – in keeping with Caravaggio's reputation for painting only from nature – are largely based on studies from life, though the kneeling boy in the center and his horse were inspired by figures

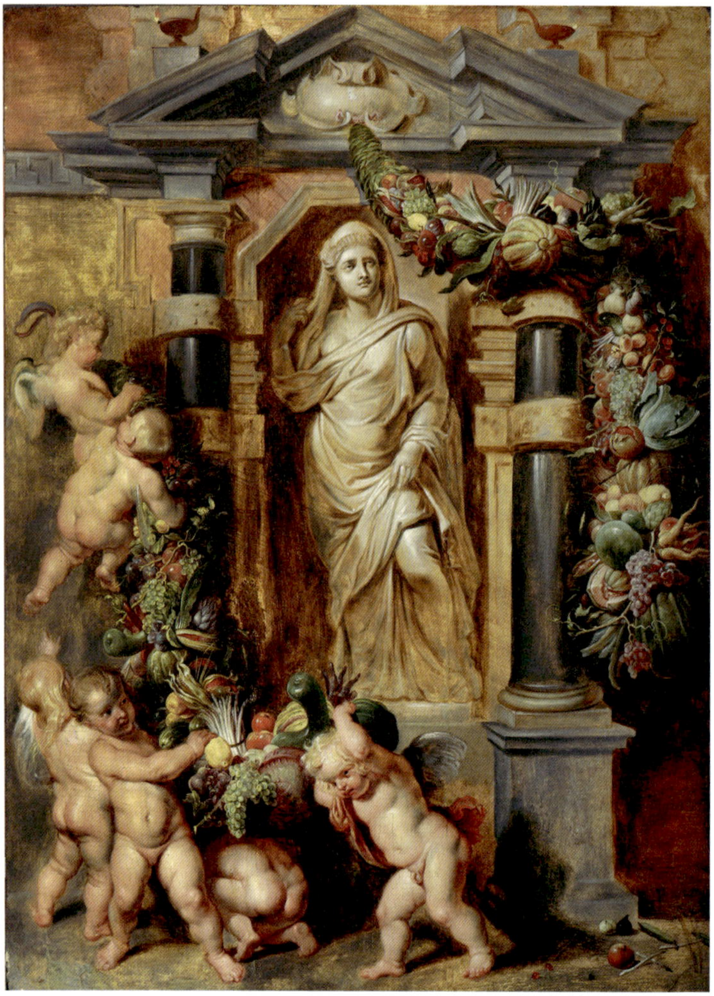

9. Peter Paul Rubens, *Homage to Ceres,* ca. 1614–15, Lucerne, Collection Hermann Alexander Beyeler, oil on panel, 91 × 66 cm

10. Jacques Jordaens, *Achelous Defeated by Hercules,* 1649, Copenhagen, Statens Museum for Kunst, oil on canvas, 245 × 311 cm, inv. KMSsp233

from Bassano's *Winter.* This too is probably no accident, for the passage in Virgil's *Georgics* that most evokes Jordaens's invention refers specifically to the changing of the seasons: "Above all, worship the gods, and pay great Ceres her yearly rites, sacrificing on the glad sward, with winter's last days, when clear springtime is now come.... Then let all your country folk worship Ceres."[17] This too may explain why Jordaens also looked to a Madonna for inspiration: although we tend to associate Ceres with the autumn harvest, she is explicitly associated with springtime in the passage just cited – the season that also brings the Easter and the resurrection of Christ, who is also referred to as God's first fruits.[18] Jordaens's lively invention stands in stark contrast to Rubens's earlier *Homage to Ceres* of ca. 1614–15 (fig. 9; Beyeler version),[19] whose stony aspect he explicitly rejects in favor of flesh and blood – entirely in keeping with Rubens's own art theoretical advice, which holds that though painters should imitate the

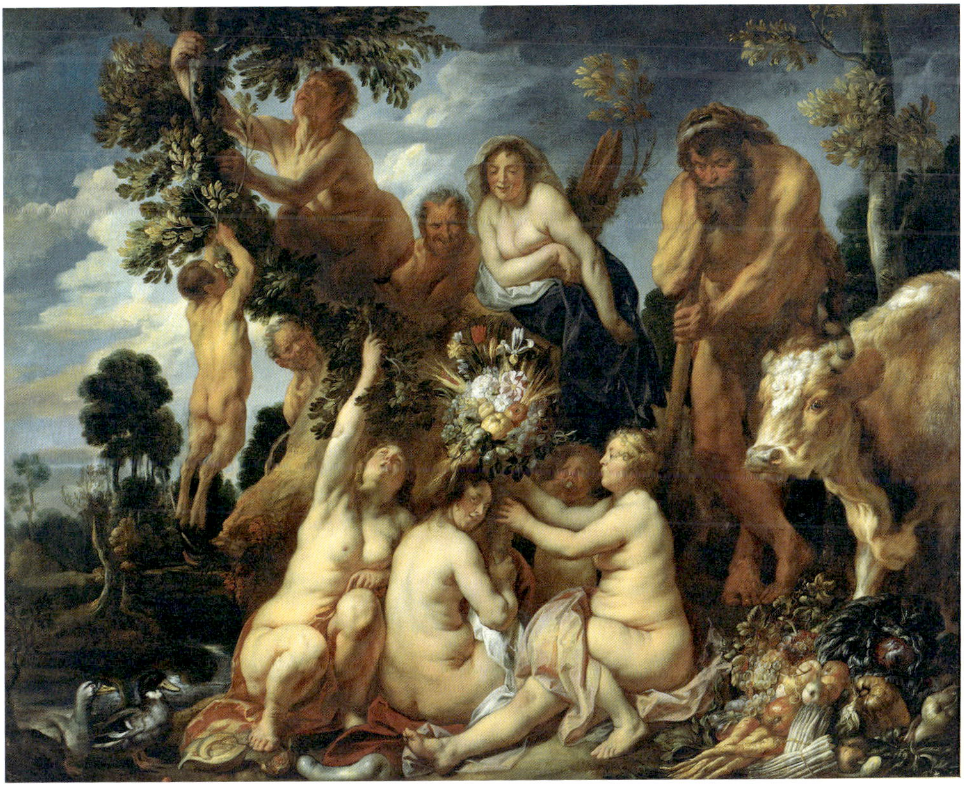

statuary of antiquity, it should never have the appearance of stone.[20]

Later allegories of Abundance by Jordaens elaborate on his earlier inventions of the 1610s and 20s. They may also have been meant to hark back deliberately to ancient Roman tradition, in which peace, or Pax, was inextricably associated with the fertility of the earth (Ubertas) and generosity of rulers (Liberalitas).[21] At least, this is what their monumental scale suggests when read in light of their early provenance and date of production. Jordaens's *Achelous Defeated by Hercules* (fig. 10), for example, may have been commissioned by Christian IV of Denmark (Koester 143) to commemorate the signing of the Treaty of Münster in 1648.[22] The painting is dated 1649 and was shipped from Antwerp to Denmark via Holland in 1652 or early 1653.

The *Allegory of Abundance* now in Dresden (fig. 11), painted around the same time, is almost exactly the same size as its counterpart in Copenhagen, and it is tempting to view the two as pendants.[23] Not only do they share the same non-standard format and exuberant style, they also represent consecutive episodes in the story of Cornucopia's origins: the victory of Hercules, and the subsequent offering of Achelous's horn to Bona Copia. Indeed, in the Dresden canvas Bona Copia appears to be the living embodiment of a well-fleshed Roman goddess of fertility, such as Bona Dea or Ops. However, it is unlikely to have been sold as a pendant to the Copenhagen canvas,

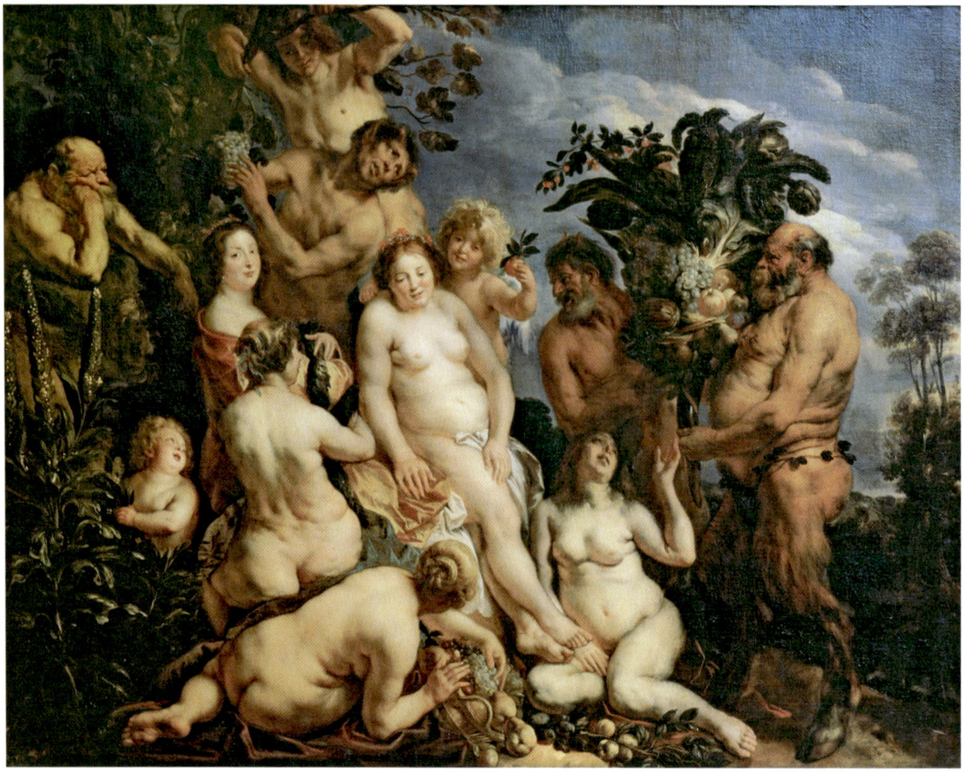

11. Jacques Jordaens, *Allegory of Abundance,* ca. 1648–49, Dresden, Gemäldegalerie Alte Meister, Staatliche Kunstsammlungen, oil on canvas, 240 × 315 cm, inv. 1009

as it was only acquired for the Saxon royal collections in 1709, when it was purchased from an art dealer in Antwerp. It is more likely that in the course of the (presumed) Danish commission, Jordaens painted more than one variation on the same theme in order to provide his patron with a range of choices, the remainder of which he could sell to other buyers if need be – as he is known to have done in the context of other commissions.[24]

This hypothesis is further reinforced by the existence of several composition drawings depicting the same or very closely related subjects, among them the comparatively large, highly finished watercolor of *Achelous Defeated by Hercules* now in Brussels (fig. 12),[25] which may have been a *modello* for or *ricordo* of its painted counterpart in Copenhagen.

For all that Jordaens exulted in painting the pleasures of plenty for their own sake, the very notion of *copia* was laden with art-theoretical significance. In chapter v of the *Grondt der Edel vry Schilder-const*, which deals with "ordonnantie" or the ordering of a composition, Van Mander compares the painter's task with that of

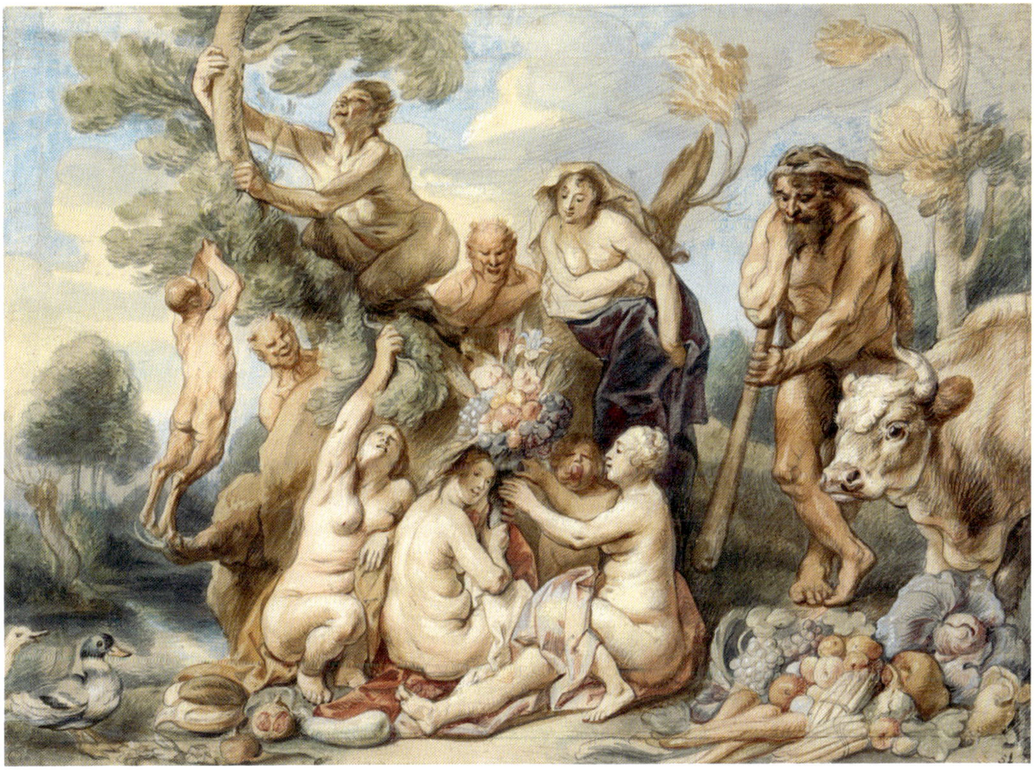

12. Jacques Jordaens, *Achelous Defeated by Hercules,* ca. 1648–49, Brussels, RMFAB, black chalk and watercolor, some body color, 306 × 433 mm, inv. 4060/1655

a wise patriarch. Order is a fundamental quality of the universe: "both in God's creation, high and low, and kingdoms, countries, city-states, families, and the various disciplines created by inventive people."[26] The upholding of good order is closely allied to the control of *copia*, or abundance. A little further on, Van Mander advises the painter to limit the number of figures he uses to tell a story, in imitation of "great majesties: kings or powerful potentates, who do not put forward a great deal of talk, but either orally or with the pen make their opinions known with few words." The example of lawyers – who use too many words in pleading their case – is strongly advised against.[27] The painter should learn from Varro, who limited the number of guests at his table to nine or ten in order to avoid excess noise or any other unseemliness that would interfere with conversation and true conviviality.[28] Jordaens clearly abuses this advice to good effect in works like *The King Drinks* and *As the Old Sing, So the Young Pipe,* which play on the perceived link between domestic microcosm and political macrocosm, as a disorderly household was often considered a metaphor for a poorly run state. Elsewhere, in subjects having little to do with domestic discipline, Jordaens may have sought to lend additional art-theoretical backbone to his compositions by stuffing them with figures and objects, thereby exploiting the visual pleasures and the charged meaning of the chaotic surface.[29] In this way the paintings themselves become veritable cornucopias, filled with messages from the gods.

In light of the art-theoretical link between *copia* and chaos – so useful to Jordaens in making a point about the political hazards of the world turned upside down – there is something poignant about his allegories of fertility and abundance, which deliberately evoke the order of the cosmos. As the passages from Virgil in particular reveal, the decorum of gods and stars appropriate to each season governs the passing of time and affairs of men. Jordaens would explore this idea more explicitly in the series of twelve signs of the Zodiac he painted for the ceiling of his own house, which offered no panoramic vistas to the street as did Rubens's splendid palazzo on the Meir.[30] While perhaps just as opulent, Jordaens's eclectic collection of houses were joined to form a single compound around an interior courtyard with limited access to the street.[31] In essence, the only way to look was inward – or upward, towards the heavens. Certainly, the motions of the stars still played a significant part in the lives of Jordaens and contemporaries – particularly among the educated. Surviving almanacs from the period, which list the rise and fall of the stars, phases of the moon, ebb and flow of the tide, and transit of the various signs of the zodiac, are often peppered with handwritten annotations confirming the truth of a particular prediction, or marking an occurrence with personal significance.[32] In a general way one might look for a similar significance in Jordaens's fascination with fertility and abundance, and with the regulation of *copia* in his oeuvre. Jordaens was baptized on May 15, 1593, and his own sign of the zodiac – Taurus, the bull – formed part of the series mentioned above. It moreover features a playful allusion to the *Rape of Europa,* in which Jupiter disguised as a white bull makes off with the eponymous princess. The rather plain Europa bears a striking resemblance to Jordaens's early portraits of his wife, Catherine van Noort – she even wears a yellow dress similar to the one in *Self-Portrait with the Van Noort* family of ca. 1616, widely regarded as a commemoration of their engagement.[33] She appears again as one of Europa's bejeweled attendants in Jordaens's *Rape of Europa,* painted around the same time.[34] It is as if Jordaens meant to suggest that she too – herself a painter's daughter – was carried away by his artistic fecundity. From the bull Zeus, the bull Achelous is but a short step away; both signal the painter's personal fascination with Nature's abundance and the fruitfulness of the divine.

[1] Virgil, *Georgics,* I, 6–12.
[2] Ovid, *Metamorphoses,* IX, 87–88.
[3] Miami Beach, Florida, Bass Museum of Art, oil on panel, 64 × 76 cm, inv. 79.275; see Antwerp 1993, I, cat. A4, pp. 48–50, with reference to earlier literature.
[4] Karel van Mander, *Het Schilder-boeck* (facsimile of the 1st edition, Haarlem, 1604; Davaco Publishers, Utrecht, 1969), available online via the Databank Nederlandse Literatuur at http://www.dbnl.org/tekst/man001schi01_01 (accessed November 4, 2013). For a study of Jordaens's Ovidian subjects, see Van Eldere 1992.
[5] Oil on panel, inv. 2606. Jordaens would later copy this composition in its entirety in a drawing (Frankfurt, Städel Museum, Graphische Sammlung, watercolor over red and black chalk, wash and white highlights, 195 × 281 mm, inv. 3482).
[6] Caramulo, Portugal, Museu do Caramulo, Fundação Abel e João de Lacerda, oil on canvas, 200 × 270 cm, inv. FAL 334. The painting was made after Rubens's design for the decoration of the Torre de la Parada, 1638.
[7] Van Mander, *Wtlegginge* (as in n. 3), 73r, "nae 't ghetuyghenis van *Plutarchus* … Den hoorn (seght onsen Poeet) werdt stracx ghevult met Appelen, en alderly wel-rieckende dinghen."
[8] *Der Neue Pauly* 3, col. 160 (on Copia), and 12/1, col. 960–61 (on Ubertas).
[9] Van Mander, *Wtlegginge* (as in n. 3), 72v, 73r-v.
[10] Ibid.
[11] Munich, Bayrische Staatsgemäldesammlungen, Alte Pinakothek, oil on canvas, 250 × 240 cm, inv. 10411.
[12] Vienna, Sammlung des Regierenden Fürsten von Liechtenstein, Vaduz, 217.8 × 317.3 cm, inv. GE 111.
[13] On Rubens's learned invention, see A. Georgievska-Shine, "From Ovid's Cecrops to Rubens's City of God in the *Finding of Ericthonius,*" *Art Bulletin* 86 (2004), pp. 58–74; see also E. McGrath, "Garlanding the Great Mother: Rubens, Jan Brueghel and the Celebration of Nature's Fertility," *Munuscula Amicorum: Contributions on Rubens and his Colleagues in Honour of Hans Vlieghe,* pp. 103–22. On Jordaens's version of the *Finding of Ericthonius,* see R. Klessmann, "Jacob Jordaens, zur Ikonographie und Bildregie seiner Historienbilder," *Von Bruegel bis Rubens: Das goldene Jahrhundert der flämischen Malerei,* pp. 151–60.
[14] Madrid, Museo del Prado, oil on canvas, 165 × 112 cm, inv. PO15470.
[15] Jan Saenredam after Hendrick Goltzius, engraving, 450 × 323 mm, London, British Museum, inv. 1850,1214.49.
[16] Vienna, Gemäldegalerie, Kunsthistorisches Museum, oil on canvas, 364.5 × 249.5 cm, inv. GG_147.
[17] Virgil, *Georgics,* I, 338–43.
[18] Exodus 23:16, which enjoins the children of Israel to observe the festival of harvest; this passage is alluded to in 1 Corinthians 15:2à, when Christ's resurrection is said to make him "first fruits of those who have died."
[19] Lucerne, Collection Hermann Alexander Beyeler, 91 × 66 cm; see Belliny and Gritsay 2007; see also the version in St Peterburg, Hermitage, 90.5 × 65.5 cm, inv. GE 504; Gritsay and Babina 2007, pp. 23–33.
[20] See Muller 1982.
[21] See Joost Vander Auwera's remarks in Brussels/Kassel 2012, p. 168.
[22] Copenhagen, Statens Museum for Kunst, oil on canvas, 245 × 311 cm, inv. KMSsp233.
[23] Dresden, Gemäldegalerie Alte Meister, Staatliche Kunstsammlungen, oil on canvas, 240 × 315 cm, inv. 1009.
[24] N. De Poorter, "Seriewerk en recyclage: doorgedreven efficientie in het geroutineerde atelier van Jacob Jordaens," *Concept, Design and Execution in Flemish Painting (1550–1700),* pp. 213–32.
[25] Brussels, RMFAB, black chalk and watercolor, some body color, 306 × 433 mm, inv. 4060/1655.
[26] Van Mander, *Grondt,* I, v, 1, 126; vol. II, 461.
[27] Van Mander, *Grondt,* I, v, 27-28, 137; see also II, 474.
[28] Van Mander, *Grondt,* I, v, 29-31, 137; see also II, 474–75.
[29] [*Grondt,* V, 61, I, 146; II, 485].
[30] These paintings now decorate the ceiling of the Bibliothèque du Sénat in the Palais du Luxembourg; they measure approximately 164.5 × 124.5 cm, with variations; see Antwerp 1993, I, p. 258, under cats A84–A86, II, p. 74, under cat. B47, and U. Moussalli, "Un chef-d'oeuvre inconnu. Les douze signes du zodiaque de Jacques Jordaens," *Le Jardin des Arts* (1956), pp. 660–67.
[31] On Jordaens's house, see Tijs 1984.
[32] Several such exemplars can be found in the Bibliotheek Hendrik Conscience in Antwerp.
[33] Museumslandschaft Hessen Kassel, Gemäldegalerie Alte Meister, oil on canvas, 130.5 × 159 cm, inv. GK 107; for a dissenting opinion see Büttner 2010, pp. 17–19.
[34] Gemäldegalerie, Staatliche Museen zu Berlin, oil on canvas, 173 × 235 cm.

The Evolution of an *Allegory of Fruitfulness*

LUCY DAVIS

Jordaens's *Allegory of Fruitfulness* in the Wallace Collection is a very rare example of a mythological painting by the Flemish master in a British public collection (*Allegory of Fruitfulness*, pp. 12–13).[1] Jordaens painted the subject twice: another version is at the Royal Museums of Fine Arts of Belgium in Brussels (*Allegory of Fertility*, pp. 6–7). The two works have some immediately obvious differences, however. Most strikingly, the woman holding the cornucopia is seen from the front in the former and from the back in the latter. The relationship between the two versions has long puzzled art historians. The aim of this study is to present new insights into the development of the composition of the Wallace Collection picture and its relationship with the Brussels version.

The Wallace Collection's painting was acquired by Sir Richard Wallace, son of the 4th Marquess of Hertford, in 1872.[2] The composition shows a group of mostly ecstatic, bacchic figures – satyrs and humans of various ages – gathered around a frontally posed, semi-nude nymph, who holds up a vast cornucopia that dominates the composition. The woman in red proffers even more fruit, which she holds in the folds of her dress. The central figure points at two children, which further suggests that the image is a celebration of fruitfulness and fecundity. The subject was once identified as a *Homage to Pomona,* the sylvan nymph who tended fruits and trees.[3] The fourteenth book of Ovid's *Metamorphoses* has been cited as a textual source for the image, which is taken to depict the arrival of Silvanus, satyrs and pans intending to pay court to the goddess.[4] Ovid does not in fact describe an actual meeting but rather describes the admiration that the woodland creatures are supposed to have shared for Pomona on account of her beauty and chastity. Joost Vander Auwera and Irene Schaudies have instead proposed that Jordaens's paintings of the theme are primarily intended to celebrate fertility and its close association with peace and abundance, and to evoke the sensual world of ancient Roman sculpture, and are not intended to depict a particular scene from any textual source. Jordaens shared Rubens's fascination for bacchic subjects and the creative freedom they afforded, and he developed a distinctive idiom in their depiction.

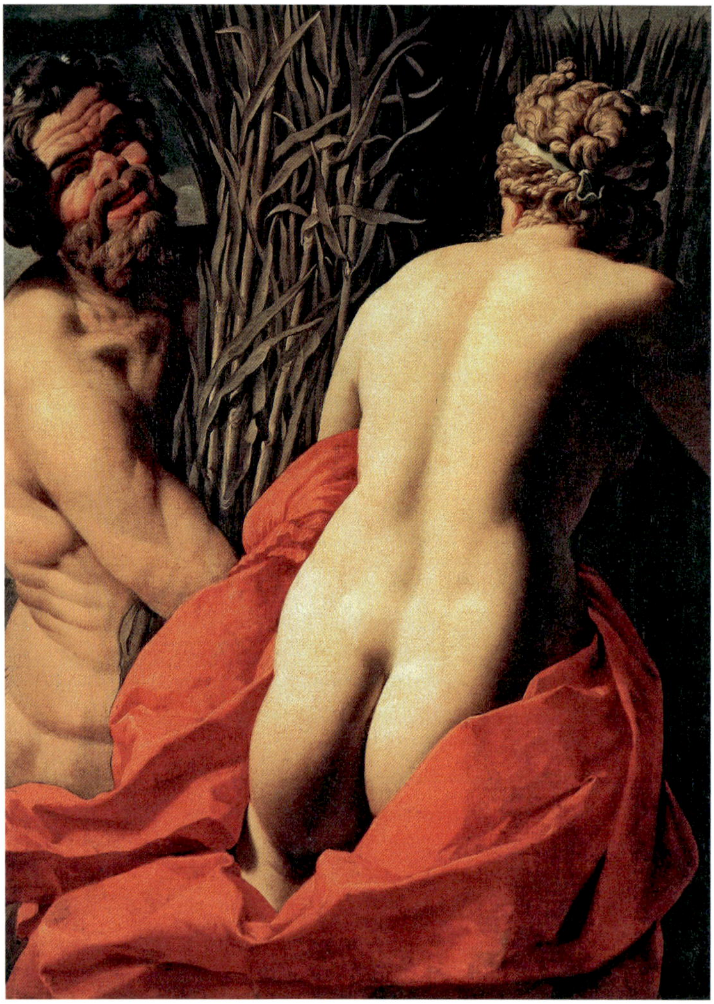

13. Abraham Janssen, *Pan and Syrinx,* ca. 1618–19, Bremen, Kunstsammlungen Böttscherstrasse, Museum im Roselius-Haus, oil on canvas, 120 × 98 cm, inv. B135

The Development of the Composition: the Relationship between the Brussels and the Wallace Collection's Versions

Despite its rarity, Jordaens's painting at the Wallace was not cleaned for generations. In 2010, it was decided to carry out much-needed conservation work in close cooperation with the Royal Museums in Brussels, seeking to examine and compare our two versions in an unprecedented technical analysis of both works. The project formed a core part of new research into Jordaens in preparation for the major exhibition *Jordaens and the Antique* held at the Royal Museums of Fine Arts of Belgium, Brussels, and the Museumslandschaft Hessen Kassel.

Prior to this work, scholars had historically sought to establish the dates and the relationship between the versions in London and Brussels by relying on largely subjective perceptions of changes in the artist's style. Perhaps unsurprisingly, they did not agree on which composition was painted first. In 1906

Max Rooses considered the Wallace Collection composition to be a later version of the Brussels picture. He dated both versions to the period 1623–25.[5] Rooses thought that the London painting was the more simple version, with the re-orientation of the central figure creating a "finer, more decorative" overall effect, but one that had lost some of its character, "sweeter but more ordinary."

According to Rooses, it was the possibility of painting the central figure from behind, rather than from the more conventional frontal view, that had first attracted Jordaens to the composition. The fascinating exhibition *Jordaens and the Antique* in 2012–13 recently demonstrated that Janssen's arresting *Pan and Syrinx,* ca. 1618–19, which is dominated by the nude Syrinx seen from behind, is likely to have posed a competitive challenge for Jordaens and his contemporaries (fig. 13).[6] For Rooses, the later reworking of the composition on the London canvas caused unresolved compositional problems: the central figure seemed no longer to interact satisfactorily with the surrounding figures and she holds up the large, heavy cornucopia with unpersuasive effortlessness.[7] Despite his less favorable qualitative judgment of the Wallace Collection's painting, Rooses did not suggest the involvement of a hand other than that of Jordaens himself.

Roger d'Hulst identified a group of compositions by Jordaens relating to the theme of fertility, and dated them to ca. 1623–25 on account of a similar grouping of figures, handling of light and shadow, and color.[8] Like Rooses, he considered the London painting to be the later version, dating the Brussels version to ca. 1623 and the Wallace version to ca. 1630–40.[9] He also raised the question of workshop involvement in the London picture, a suggestion that found some support.[10]

Others disagreed, however, with the idea that the Wallace Collection's picture was painted after the Brussels composition. In 1965 Leo van Puyvelde dated the London painting to the very beginning of Jordaens's career, 1618–20, some three years after he had matriculated from the Guild of St Luke and when he was still working with Rubens.[11] Van Puyvelde saw the Wallace Collection's painting as the tentative first effort, which preceded the Brussels composition (which he dated to ca. 1623–25) by about five years. He saw the Brussels painting as the culmination of Jordaens's engagement with the subject.

The arguments summarized above were largely predicated on the notion of a "prime version," that is to say a version of a work that represents the optimal composition in which the artist resolves compositional problems encountered in his earlier attempts. The applicability of this notion to the present case, however, has been severely challenged by recent developments in conservation and technical art history. Recent X-ray and technical analysis suggest that the relationship between the Brussels and Wallace Collection paintings was not a straightforward one and that one painting does not simply follow on from the other as a sequence of distinct versions. The X-ray shows the fully worked-up composition of the Brussels painting underneath that of the Wallace Collection's painting with the upper layers painted directly over the underlying composition, without an intermediary layer. The London painting is therefore a substantially reworked version of what actually lies underneath. The X-ray also reveals the complexity of the paint structure of the Wallace Collection's picture, which includes no less than three campaigns of painting, as discussed by Victoria Sutcliffe and Anna Sandén. In comparison, the X-ray of the Brussels painting reveals far fewer and less extensive pentimenti. This suggests that when it was put to canvas, Jordaens had already worked out the composition of the Brussels picture to his satisfaction beforehand and therefore had a very clear idea of what the end result would look like. It would therefore appear that Jordaens painted the Wallace Collection's picture first, and in so

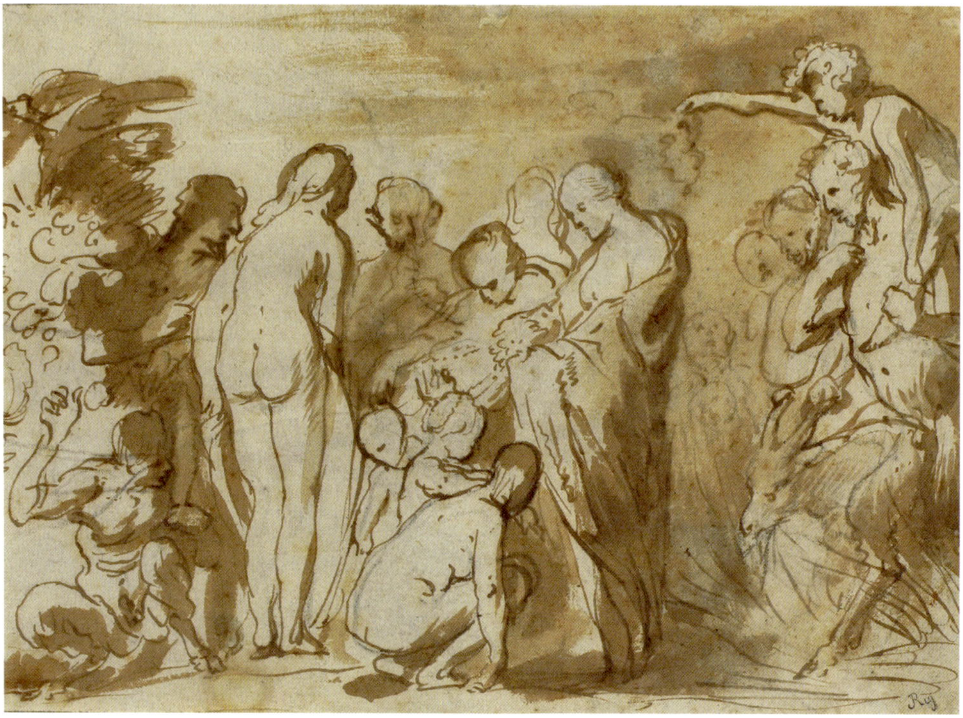

doing worked out his idea for the Brussels composition. His reuse of a canvas (which involved painting over an existing composition) could indicate that he treated the Wallace Collection canvas as a more speculative "work-in-progress" in his studio, rather than as a work he was painting on commission. Having developed the image of the woman with her back turned, he started a fresh canvas – the one in Brussels. The brushwork on the Brussels canvas is more careful and finished than it is on the London version, and the presence of a signature (absent in the London version) perhaps indicates that Jordaens was either working on commission or had a particular patron in mind.

While the Brussels picture may have left his studio very soon after its completion, the Wallace Collection's version must have remained in his studio (perhaps as a record of his successful composition), to which he appears to have returned later and substantially modified.[12] As a palimpsest composition that Jordaens probably retained for reference in his workshop, the London *Allegory of Fruitfulness* is far from unique in Jordaens's oeuvre. Other, similarly complex works, such as the composite versions of *The King Drinks*, now in Kassel, and *As the Old Sing, So the Young Pipe*, now in Munich, are built around core canvases that seem to have remained in the studio for many years, undergoing various stages of expansion and alteration.[13]

Such a working practice would be consistent with Jordaens's own declaration regarding his artistic methods. In a legal document of 1648 he testified before a notary that he had made multiple versions of compositions and kept them in the studio for long periods of time, with a view to modifying them at a later date. In this specific case, he mentioned

14. Jacques Jordaens, *Allegory of the Land's Fertility*, ca. 1623–25, Brussels, RMFAB, pen and brown ink, brown wash, partly over an initial sketch in black chalk, 191 × 261 mm, inv. 6155

15. Jacques Jordaens, *Allegory of Fertility*, ca. 1623–25, Copenhagen, National Gallery of Denmark, pen and brush in brown ink, traces of black and red chalk, 240 × 230 mm, inv. KKS10091

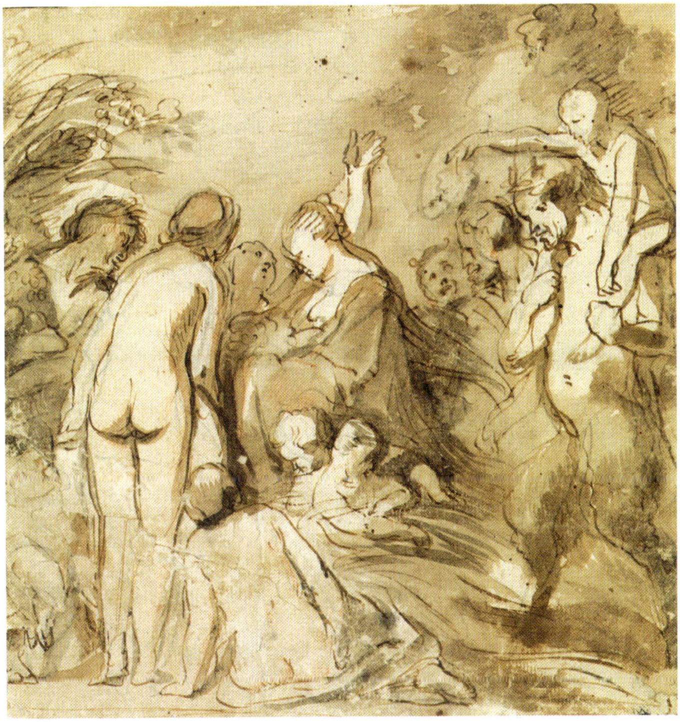

several paintings he consigned to the art dealer Martinus van Langenhoven in The Hague, including *As the Old Sing, So the Young Pipe, Candaules, Argus,* and *Vulcan*. These paintings had been copies made by his workshop assistants, which he then retouched and modified to such an extent that he considered them to be his own work.[14]

The document of 1648 also touches on the question of workshop participation, which was also raised by d'Hulst in his study (see above). The painting does indeed have an uneven quality to it, due to the fact that some of the reworked areas are very thinly painted in comparison with the built-up paint layers of the unaltered figures, such as the old satyr carrying the young satyr. The thinness of paint is particularly evident in the figure of the old satyr or Silenus in the center, which has a rather flat appearance. The pentimenti are perhaps more clearly visible to the eye today due to the deterioration of pigments, but it seems that Jordaens allowed his reformulations to remain visible in the revised version. The summarily painted forearm of the woman in red is also very rapidly painted over the red of her dress, with little modeling. In the central figure, the ochre waves of her hair (of her originally turned head) are left exposed, perhaps deliberately, in order to serve as rough contours of the bone structure of the side of her face. The straight highlights of the leg, originally intended as those of her calves, remain to serve the same function for her shins but with a rather abrupt and unmodified effect. The rapid, even cursory execution in the revisions does not however indicate the hand of a workshop assistant, who would probably do his utmost to ensure that any work entrusted to him by his master would be executed to meet a high standard of diligence. Furthermore, as John Ingamells pointed out in 1992, the pentimenti are too extensive for a workshop replica.[15] Jordaens may even have left them visible as a demonstration of his artistic virtuosity.

The absence of a direct preparatory drawing for the Wallace Collection's composition (visible today) also supports the theory that Jordaens thought out the changes to his painting directly on the canvas. The two extant preparatory drawings, in Brussels and Copenhagen, are both fundamental compositional studies for the two Allegories of Fruitfulness but do not account for such changes as the reversal of the central figure and the overpainting of the satyr supporting the cornucopia (figs. 14–15).

The Meaning of the Pentimenti

The satyr carrying the child on his shoulders, the piping figure, the woman who carries fruit in the folds of her dress, the child who pulls at the irises, the young woman seated on the ground and her male companion are all present, with modifications, in both the Brussels and London versions of the subject. The most extensive revision, as already mentioned, was the reorientation of the central figure. While in the Brussels painting she looks inwards to receive the gifts from her acolytes, in the Wallace Collection's composition she turns outwards. The old satyr behind her who held the top of the cornucopia (Brussels) has been painted out, so that the cornucopia is now supported at the top by the maenad herself, and at its base by the crouching satyr at her feet. As Rooses pointed out, however, neither figure convincingly bears any of its notional weight, which must be considerable.

The maenad in the final painting is posed for the viewer and her emphatic pointing gesture leads us directly to the new focus of the composition: the two children at her feet. The little girl was alone in the earlier composition but here she is joined by a little boy, who is her equal in age and height. She looks down and forwards while he looks back up at the maenad. Their torsos and arms interlock as together they pull back the irises; the backs of their heads are joined as their faces are turned in either direction like a Janus-head. This particular motif was frequently used by Rubens in his bacchic compositions, and is very effectively deployed here to transform the children into a pair of twins – twins, or Gemini, were the zodiac sign for the blossoming spring month of May and frequently used in art to personify that month (perhaps not coincidentally, the month in which Jordaens was born, though probably under the sign of Taurus, the bull, with which the month begins).[16]

Sensual love, suggested in the earlier composition, is more forcefully invoked through the revisions to the young man and woman in the foreground. Jordaens increases the erotic charge by transforming the crouching boy into a satyr with goat's hooves, and by having the girl raise her head to meet his lusty gaze. In the Brussels version she looked down. Now that she looks up, the grapes she holds seem to take on a greater symbolic importance and thus provide a commentary on the interaction. Joost Vander Auwera has plausibly shown that a bunch of grapes held up delicately at the stem between forefinger and thumb was used in seventeenth-century emblematic culture as an allegory of virginity.[17]

The woman in the red dress was also changed extensively in the second campaign of painting. In the original version, she was older, a mature woman with a "matronly" build. Her (clothed) upper torso was turned towards the picture plane, with both arms holding up the fruit in the folds of her drapery. In the final version, she was entirely repainted as a younger woman with a slimmer body and distinctly Rubensian facial type, and reoriented to stand at right angles to the

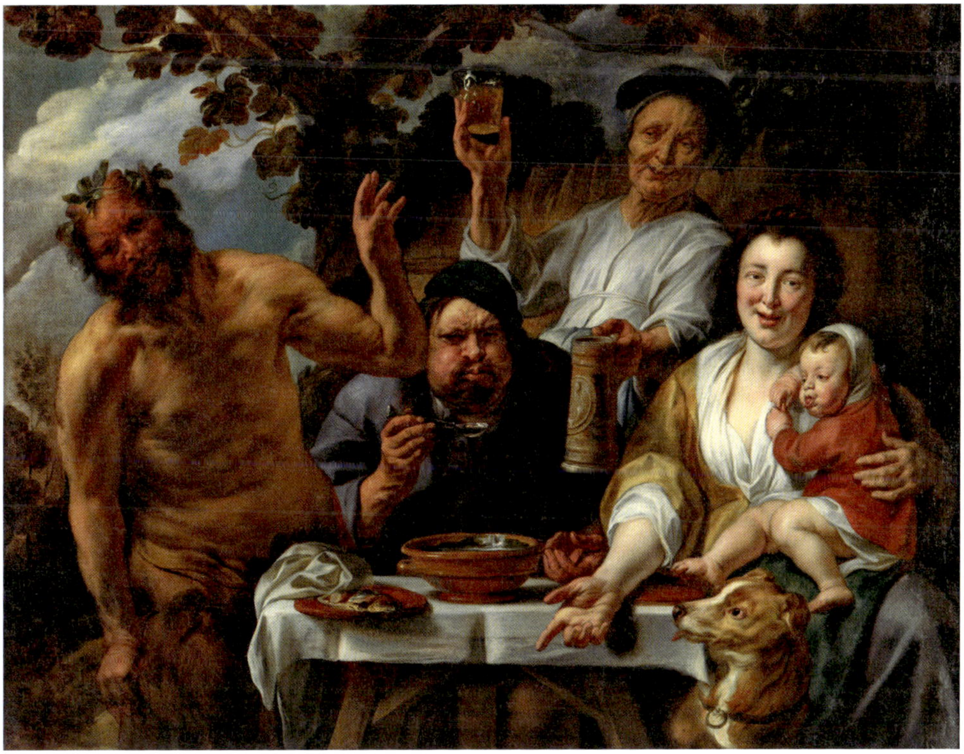

16. Jacques Jordaens, *Satyr and Peasant*, ca. 1645, Brussels, RMFAB, oil on canvas, 130 × 172 cm, inv. 588

picture plane with one breast exposed. She is now also the appropriate age to be the youthful Pomona, "a virgin of the sylvan train" (until her encounter with Vertumnus) whom she resembles in the act of protecting fruit in the drapery of her dress.[18] However, Pomona was traditionally depicted fully clad in order to emphasize her chastity.

In the final composition, a grinning old satyr has replaced the young woman reaching for grapes, standing between the woman in red and the maenad. Perhaps Jordaens included him as a nod to the episode in Ovid's *Metamorphoses* in which Silenus, foster father to the wine god Bacchus, turns up uninvited to pay homage to the earth goddess Cybele with the satyrs and nymphs.[20] Jordaens may also have included him to allude to the series of satyrs and peasants he was painting, possibly around this time (see the following section). In the context of an allegory of fertility, Silenus serves as a counterpoint (or "contrapposto") to the youth and beauty of the central female figures; as an old satyr, he was also an important component of the bacchanal that, by convention, represented the ages of man. The black celebrant has been modified slightly in order to play the panpipes, the wind instrument closely associated with the chaotic and unbridled bacchic world. The old satyr on the right has remained largely unchanged, but the boy he carries on his shoulders has acquired the horns and pointed ears of a little satyr.

The changes made between the original (known to us through the Brussels version) and the final version (in the composition we now see at the Wallace Collection) indicate that Jordaens revised his composition to make it more bacchic in flavor, and to emphasize human fecundity in the midst of Nature's omnipresent fruitfulness and abundance.

Dating of the Wallace Collection *Allegory of Fruitfulness*

The X-ray taken in 2012 revealed that the Brussels composition lies under the Wallace Collection's painting. Although neither work is securely dated, the Brussels painting has been unanimously dated to ca. 1623–25 on stylistic grounds. For the reasons outlined above, it seems plausible that the underlying composition of the London picture was painted first, that is, before ca. 1623. When was the second campaign of painting completed – that is, the composition we see today? The unevenness of execution across the Wallace Collection's painting makes it particularly difficult to date the revisions, which may in any case have been painted incrementally, rather than in a single campaign.[20] Furthermore, Jordaens remains an artist whose oeuvre is difficult to arrange in an order that corresponds to a linear stylistic development.

The inclusion of the frontally oriented Silenus recalls both in compositional and stylistic terms two paintings from the early 1640s. The first is the *Flora, Silenus, and Zephyr* (Berlin, private collection), ca. 1640–45, in which Silenus is placed between two central figures in a similar configuration as the *Allegory of Fruitfulness.* The same thinness and fluidity of the brushwork is found in the Silenus and is repeated in the *Satyr and Peasant* of ca. 1645 in the Royal Museums of Fine Arts of Belgium, Brussels (fig. 16). The satyr's raised arm, here used as a gesture of disparagement directed at his companions, is reformulated in the Wallace Collection's picture as the Silenus reaches up for the grapes.

The "Rubensian" handling of the head of the woman bearing fruit could point to either the beginning of Jordaens's career, when the women in his *Allegory of Fertility* (Munich), dated to 1616–17, recall Rubens, but so do the more refined female figures in his small cabinet paintings of ca. 1640, following Rubens's death, which focused on the female nude for the first time in his career. It was also around this time (in 1639) that Jordaens painted a series of canvases representing the story of Cupid and Psyche, which (unknown to Jordaens) although commissioned by Abate Scaglia, were ultimately intended for the Queen's House in Greenwich. As the commission progressed, Scaglia was put under increasing pressure from Charles I's agent Balthazar Gerbier, who had originally favored Rubens for the commission. Scaglia was asked to remind Jordaens of the need "to make the faces of the women as beautiful as can be, the figures more gracious and svelta [slender]."[21] This was an episode in Jordaens's career when he was under pressure to emulate Rubens, whom the English patrons held to be the great master of the female nude.

To conclude, it has been proposed that the complex structure of the Wallace Collection's painting reveals an important insight into Jordaens's creative process. The evidence provided by the technical analysis suggests that the underlying composition was begun before the Brussels painting, and largely repainted sometime after the Brussels canvas was completed, at some point between ca. 1625 and 1640.

[1] J. Ingamells, *The Wallace Collection Catalogue of Pictures, IV. Dutch and Flemish* (London, 1992), pp. 183–85.

[2] Ingamells 1992, pp. 183–85. Research into the provenance of the painting before its acquisition by Sir Richard Wallace is ongoing.

[3] D'Hulst 1952, pp. 19–31; d'Hulst 1974, I, p. 156; d'Hulst 1982, p. 107. John Ingamells, author of the Wallace Collection's 1992 catalogue, found this interpretation plausible and identified the maenad holding the cornucopia as Pomona.

[4] Ovid, *Metamorphoses*, XIV, 623–771.

[5] Rooses 1906, p. 46; Ingamells 1992, p. 184.

[6] Brussels/Kassel 2012, cat. 34, p. 96.

[7] Rooses 1906, p. 46.

[8] D'Hulst 1952, pp. 19–31, esp. 19.

[9] D'Hulst 1952, p. 19, discusses the *Homage to Ceres* (Prado), the *Allegory of Fertility* (Munich and Brussels), and the Wallace Collection's *Allegory of Fruitfulness* as a discrete group in Jordaens's oeuvre.

[10] W. Laureyssens, *Jacob Jordaens in de Koninklijke Musea voor Schone Kunsten van België*, Brussels 1993, p. 46.

[11] L. van Puyvelde in *Le Siècle de Rubens*, exh. cat. Brussels (Royal Museums of Fine Arts of Belgium), 1985, pp. 117–19; Irene Schaudies, "Boistrous, druncken headed imaginary gods: The bacchic bodies of Rubens and Jordaens," *Rubens and the Human Body* (forthcoming).

[12] For the role of multiple versions in the development of the image and its role in artistic process in the context of Reynolds and British art, see Alexandra Gent, Rachel Morrison, and Rica Jones, "*The Strawberry Girl*: Repetition in Reynolds's Studio Practice," Copenhagen (2011).

[13] These issues were discussed most recently at the symposium *Reframing Jordaens* (Brussels, 6–7 December 2012) in a presentation by Timo Trümper; see also K. Renger, "'Wie die Alten sungen, …' Kompositionsänderungen im Werk von Jacob Jordaens," *Kunst und Antiquitäten* 4 (1989), pp. 52–58, and X. Egorova, "Changements autographes dans les peintures de Jordaens conservées au Musée Pouchkine de Moscou (d'après les examens radiographiques)," *Jaarboek Koninklijk Museum voor Schone Kunsten Antwerpen* (1993), pp. 165–85.

[14] Antwerp 1993, I, p. 14.

[15] Ingamells 1992, pp. 183–85.

[16] See for example, the Janus-headed supporting figure that stands immediately behind Silenus in the *Drunken Silenus*, Alte Pinakothek, Munich. I would like to thank Joost Vander Auwera for this suggestion.

[17] Joost Vander Auwera in Brussels/Kassel 2012, p. 175.

[18] Ovid, *Metamorphoses* XIV, 623–24.

[19] Ovid, *Fasti* VI, 319.

[20] See essay in this volume by Joost Vander Auwera.

[21] E. McGrath, *Jordaens, Psyche, and the Abbot: Myth, Decorum, and Italian Manners in Seventeenth-Century Antwerp* (Groningen, 2009), pp. 1–48, esp. 10–11.

Jordaens's *Allegory of Fertility*: The History and Creation of a Masterpiece

JOOST VANDER AUWERA

Positioning a Masterpiece in the Museum's Collection

The *Allegory of (the Earth's) Fertility*[1] (pp. 6–7), is one of the very first works by Jordaens that did not end up in the Brussels museum by virtue of historical accident; rather, it was purchased deliberately. Before 1827, the museum had only managed to acquire one Jordaens on its own initiative. At that time the museum, created by Napoleon Bonaparte as the Musée départemental de la Dyle in 1801, was still under the jurisdiction of the city of Brussels rather than the Belgian state.[2] In 1809, the institution purchased a preparatory oil sketch for *The Triumph of Prince Frederik Hendrik of Nassau (1584–1647)* from the Parisian revolutionary painter Anicet Charles Gabriel Lemonnier (1743–1824).[3] When the museum brought out the highest bid on the *Allegory of Fertility* at the sale of the collection of Baron de Vinck d'Orp on May 28, 1827,[4] it did possess a *Bust of an Apostle,* but the latter was attributed to Van Dyck, not Jordaens.[5] Nor was it purchased deliberately: it was found in a depot abandoned by the French at the end of the eighteenth century after they had conquered the Austrian Netherlands and transported the most desirable artworks to the Louvre. The history of the monumental *Saint Martin Healing a Possessed Man* is similar:[6] formerly it adorned the main altar of Saint Martin's Abbey in Tournai; after a relatively brief sojourn in the Louvre, it was assigned to the museum by the French government in 1811, in part thanks to pressure from local art-lovers in Brussels, in part as a gesture on the part of the French to stimulate the artistic life of the city.[7]

The early purchase of the *Allegory of Fertility* is also noteworthy in that Jordaens had fallen almost entirely from grace among the art critics and art market of the period. From the second quarter of the eighteenth century until the appearance of Max Rooses' major Jordaens monograph in 1906, his work rated low prices and interest in his art among amateurs and professionals was minimal.[8] Nevertheless, even during this period of decreased popularity, the painting did not go unnoticed. In 1852 the well-known archivist P. Génard noted its provenance in the collection and sale of J. F. de Vinck de Wezel on April 27, 1813.[9] It also featured

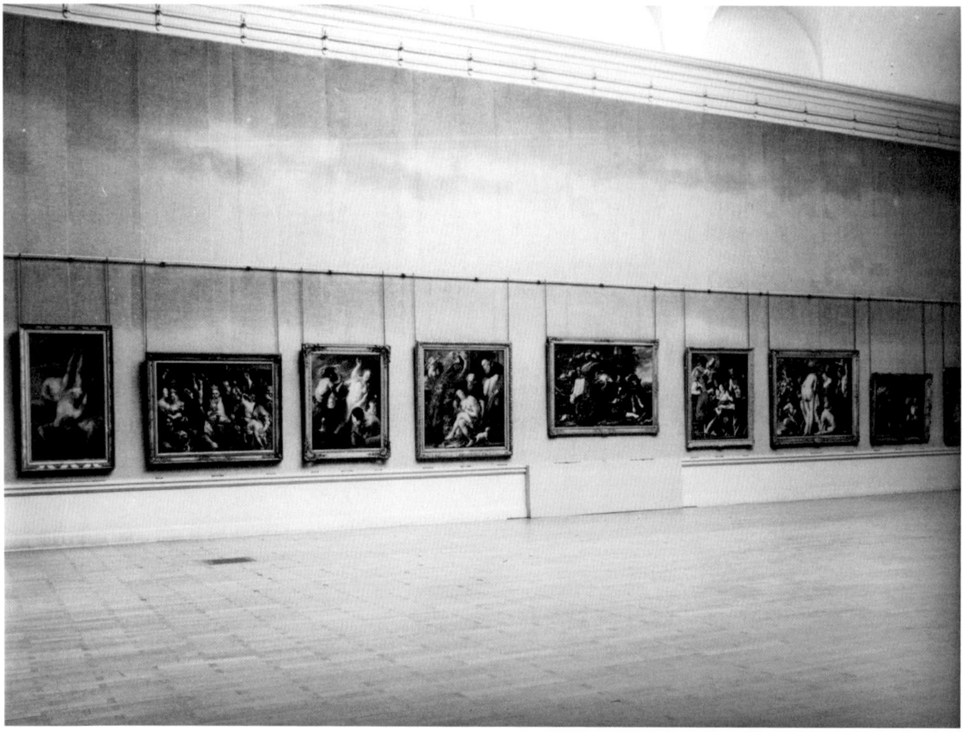

17. View of the exhibition room with the Jordaens works before February 1, 1974, RMFAB archives, photo KIK/IRPA, no. 111424N

in the first comprehensive and groundbreaking Jordaens monograph by Max Rooses in 1906.[10]

The year previous it had already been included in the first monographic exhibition on Jordaens by Paul Buschmann Jr. in Antwerp.[11] After that, however, it was seldom lent out. In 1923[12] and 1936[13] it traveled to exhibitions in Paris, and in 1946 it went to two venues of the same exhibition in Amsterdam and Rotterdam.[14] Each of these occasions involved a survey exhibition intended to promote Belgian art abroad. The exhibition of 1928, by contrast, was a special case because it represented the first exhibition devoted to Jordaens that was organized in house.[15] From December 16 to 22, 1939, it was crowned "masterpiece of the week";[16] and in 1953 it was shifted only 500 meters away from its usual location for an exhibition of old master paintings in the Palais des Beaux-Arts.[17]

It would take nearly fifty years before the painting would travel again – this time for the second venue of the exhibition *Jordaens and the Antique,* organized by the RMFAB and the Museumslandschaft Hessen Kassel in 2013.[18] The sedentary life of the canvas in recent years has a twofold explanation. In the first place, protest against the damage incurred by works of art during travel increased, and the resistance of museum curators to frequent lending increased accordingly. Secondly, the artistic and scholarly

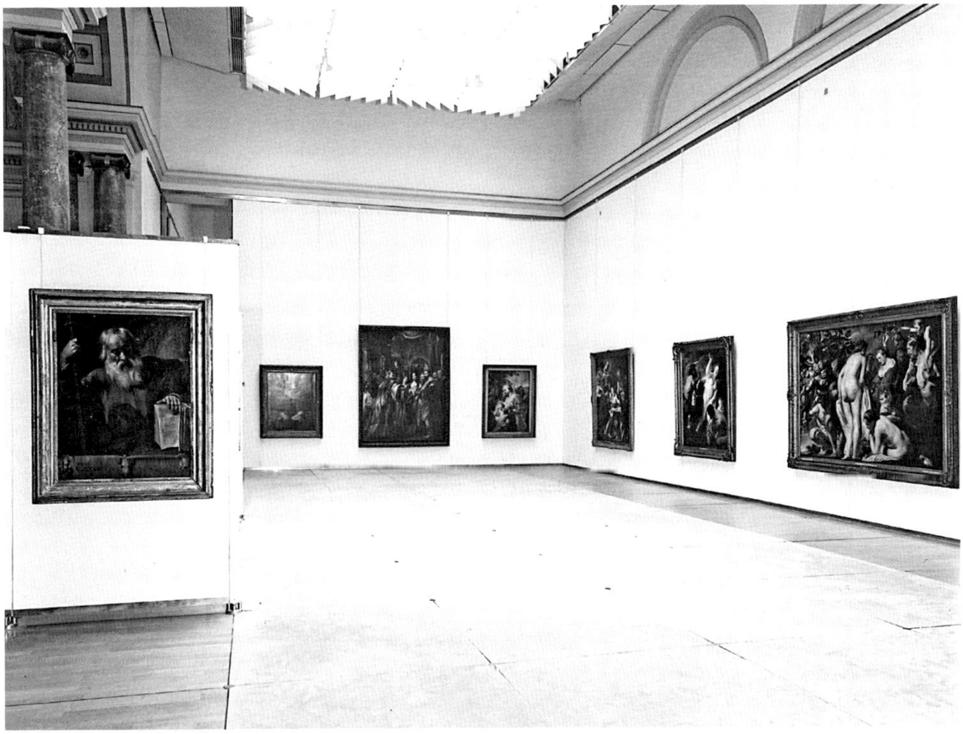

18. View of the exhibition room with the Jordaens works, January 1999, RMFAB archives, photo KIK/IRPA, no. 17750N

status of the *Allegory of Fertility* had in the meantime risen considerably. In the exhibitions of 1946 and 1953 it figured in a selection of masterpieces from Belgian public collections.[19] In 1952 the great Jordaens connoisseur R.-A. d'Hulst – then attached to the Brussels museum – chose the painting as the subject of his first article in the new *Bulletin van de Musea/Bulletin des Musées*, of which he was also the founder.[20] This new status may explain in part the heightened reserve towards – and eventual refusal of – the restoration proposed in 1966.[21] After 1974, the transformation of the *Allegory of Fertility* into one of Jordaens's absolute masterpieces translated itself into a new hanging in the exhibition rooms: previously hung in a long line of works by Jordaens (fig. 17),[22] it was given a central place in a specially installed Jordaens room (fig. 18).[23] When the painting was finally restored in 2011–12, the process was carried out under the direction of an international scientific committee. In the exhibition *Jordaens and the Antique* in 2012–13, it received a position of honor in Brussels and Kassel, and the old nationalistic myth – that the invention must somehow embody Flemish identity – was finally cast off.[24]

The Genesis of the Brussels *Allegory of Fertility*: New Methods and New Insights

In order to retrace the possible steps in the painting's creation, it is necessary to examine the various facets of artistic genesis one by one before arriving at a synthetic conclusion. First we will review the question of whether Jordaens painted the work himself, without assistants or collaborators, before investigating the role of the preparatory drawings and head studies, the function of contemporary and antique sources, the striking confidence with which the work was painted – almost without corrections or pentimenti – and finally the way in which the iconographic effectiveness and compositional logic of the painting process can be better understood in light of Jordaens's probable patron. Answers to these questions can help us to better understand how the creative processes behind the London and Brussels canvases relate to one another.

Earlier scholars came to valuable conclusions and their findings are also employed with gratitude in the discussion that follows. But they did not have at their disposal the multidisciplinary arsenal of information brought together in the recent Jordaens study published by the Universität Trier,[25] the focused exhibition in Brussels and Kassel in 2012–13, mentioned above, and the two symposia that were jointly organized by the three institutions during the course of the exhibition.[26] In addition there has been an accumulation of laboratory investigations, undertaken largely in the context of the exhibition. The canvas has been X-rayed and submitted to thread-count analysis (see essay by Don Johnson in this volume), samples of the lining have been submitted to C-14 analysis for more accurate dating, and additional analyses have been carried out on the canvas fibers and glue used to secure the lining. The painting has been thoroughly restored by Pham Thanh-Nghi with the guidance of an international scientific committee headed by Jørgen Wadum.[27] And last but not least, Anna Sandén and Victoria Sutcliffe have undertaken the first thorough restoration of the second version of the composition in the Wallace Collection in London, the results of which are likewise published in the present volume. All of these recent endeavors enable us to offer deeper and more thoroughgoing answers to the questions arising from the creation of Jordaens's masterpiece than has previously been possible.

The Role of the Workshop

In the case of art of the Ancien Régime, art history distinguishes between two sorts of collaboration between different hands: a horizontal form of collaboration, between masters of equal status, usually based on artistic specialization; and a vertical form, between a master and an assistant or assistants who are subordinate to him. They can be subordinate on various levels: not only young apprentices, but also independent masters who could not afford to acquire the (expensive) status of free master and who were either active in other workshops on a long-term basis, or offered their services on a short-term basis as journeymen – i.e. as a sort of artistic day laborer.[28] Unfortunately only the apprentices are documented more or less completely, either in the registers of the guild, or in notarial acts.[29]

The Jordaens literature dates the Brussels painting fairly unanimously to ca. 1623–25.[30] In this period Jordaens's workshop, insofar as it is documented, was not well staffed and certainly not equipped with assistants who were fully-fledged masters in their own right. In the guild year 1620–21, Charles du Val was registered as Jordaens's apprentice in the Antwerp *Liggeren*.[31] The following guild year it was Pierre de Moulyn.[32] In 1623–24 they were joined by Jan Kersgiter and Mattijs Peetersen.[33] If one assumes a normal apprenticeship period of four years, then only Du Val could have reached the appropriate level of skill to assist Jordaens in any substantial way in 1625, when

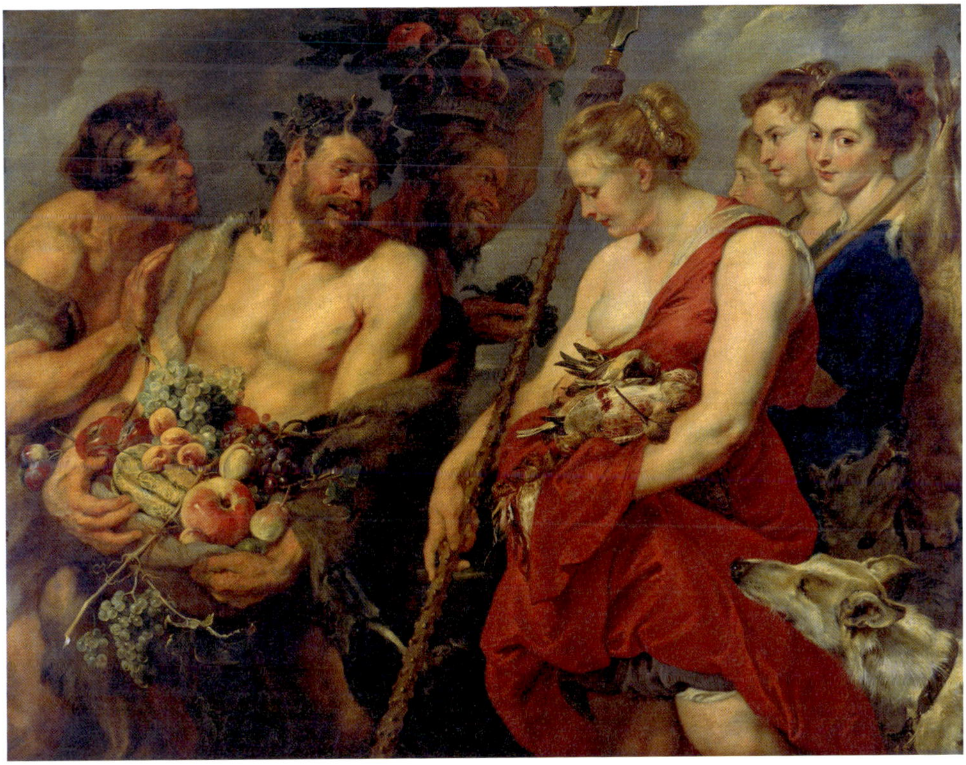

19. Peter Paul Rubens and Frans Snyders, *Diana's Return from the Hunt,* ca. 1615–16, Dresden, Gemäldegalerie Alte Meister, Staatliche Kunstsammlungen, oil on canvas, 136 × 184 cm, inv. 962A

the painting was completed.[34] More importantly, however, if one allows not only the evidence of the documents but also that of the painted surface itself to speak, nothing in the extraordinarily coherent style of the Brussels composition points in the direction of a studio assistant. Although it is true that assistants were expected to conform to the style of the master (the "trademark" of the workshop), there is nothing in this canvas that can be seen with the naked eye – either with the practiced eye of a restorer, or with the augmented eye of laboratory techniques – that betrays the involvement of another, subordinate hand.

Within the ranks of the Royal Museums in Brussels, it has long been traditional to assert that Jordaens – whose authorship of the figures has never been disputed – entered into a horizontal collaboration with Frans Snyders (1579–1657) for the considerable share of still-life elements in the composition.[35] This would form a nice parallel to the collaboration between Rubens and Snyders in paintings from ca. 1615–16, now in Dresden and Darmstadt, which are thematically similar, depicting an encounter between nymphs and satyrs (fig. 19).[36] These moreover have a similarly frieze-like composition in which the heads of the principal figures are all at approximately the same height (*isocephaly*); here too, satyrs approach from the left with fruit while the nymphs enter from the right, among whom the most prominent – in this case Diana – carries her tributes in the folds of a bright red garment, as does the principal female figure in Jordaens's invention.[37] As we shall see, however, Jordaens follows a course of his own in the present invention, combining numerous antique sources to create a splendidly balanced composition. A number of years earlier, in a painting of ca. 1615–16 now in the Bass Museum of Art in Miami Beach (fig. 1, p. 22), the influence of Rubens was more directly observable (see essay by Irene Schaudies in this volume).

The recent restoration of the Brussels painting permitted a thorough technical analysis of the canvas in its most naked form, free of varnish and overpainting. The rich collection of the Brussels museum moreover offered a unique opportunity to make direct comparisons with various paintings signed by Snyders.[38] Combined with a detailed analysis of the fluid transition between figures and still-life elements (figs. 1a–1b), it was quickly evident that the manner of execution of the fruit and vegetables, with their looser, less-detailed suggestion of form (figs. 1c–1d),[39] differed significantly from Snyders' closed forms and textures (figs. 20, 20a, 21, 21a), while it is entirely consistent with Jordaens's hand as observed in the figures. This conclusion agrees moreover with the elaboration of two drawings, one in Copenhagen (fig. 15, p. 39) and one in Brussels (fig. 14, p. 38), which the early Jordaens literature links directly with the painting in Brussels, and in which Jordaens's hand is evident in both the figures and still-life elements.[40]

The Role of the Drawings

In her essay on the painted variant in the Wallace Collection, Lucy Davis rightly notes that Jordaens's search for a suitable composition was primarily carried out by means of painting directly on canvas. This experimentation would explain the complex genesis of the London painting in at least three different phases of creation. The canvas probably remained in Jordaens's workshop for a long time and was never intended for sale. The Brussels composition was the chief beneficiary of this process, as Jordaens was able to paint it in a short time and in one go, as it were, and probably for a specific patron. Davis's arguments, which are also based on archival evidence containing Jordaens's own declarations, are quite convincing. The Brussels painting does indeed show very few signs of having been altered during painting – as we shall see later in more detail. As for the existence of a specific patron for the Brussels composition, we will present additional arguments below.

In spite of Jordaens's demonstrated penchant for seeking solutions directly on the canvas (see essay by Lucy Davis in this volume) the sheets in Copenhagen (fig. 15, p. 39) and Brussels (fig. 14, p. 38) played a definite role in the preparation of both the London and the Brussels painting. Because of their exploratory character in the use of different motifs and variations on different compositional solutions, these drawings can in no way be interpreted as *ricordi* – records of finished compositions kept in the studio for future reference. The format of the Copenhagen sheet, for example, has a format that is roughly square, like the London canvas,[41] while the sheet in Brussels is more oblong, like its painted counterpart. In the latter sheet, Jordaens also plays with the breadth of the composition by leaving more space to the right of the woman with grapes in her lap, without adopting this solution in the finished painting (yet another argument against the idea that the drawing was meant as a *ricordo*). The early date suggested by the watermark on the Brussels sheet, ca. 1596,[42] only strengthens the hypothesis that

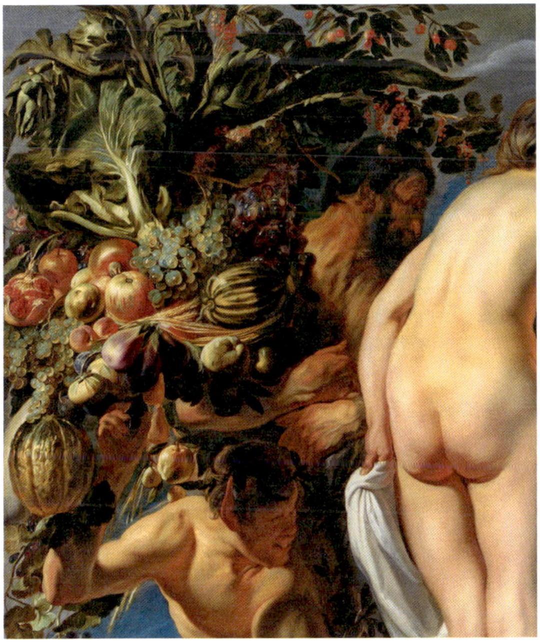

a.

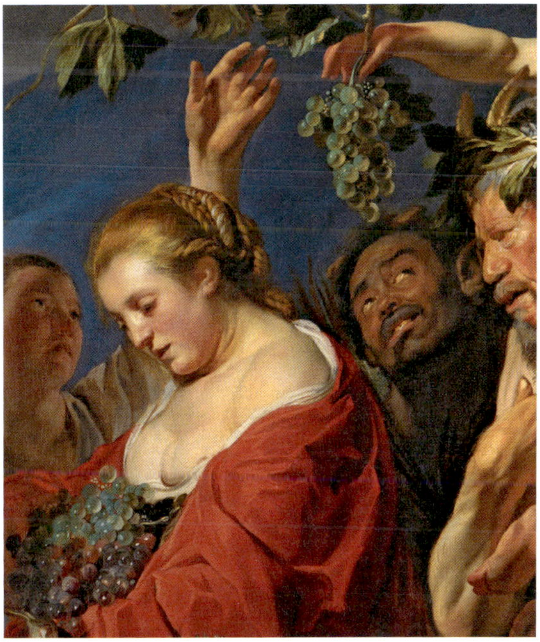

b.

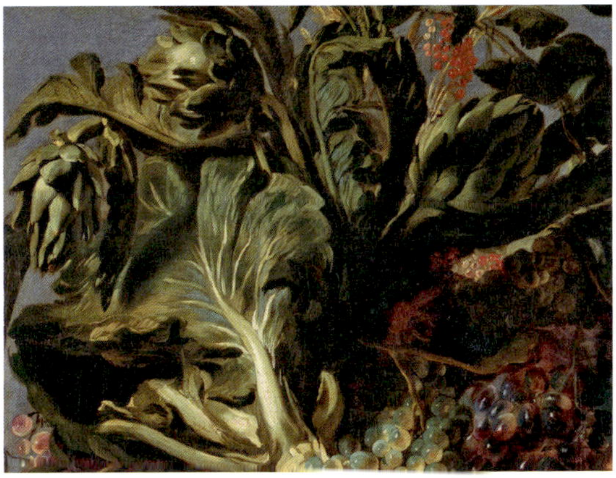

c.

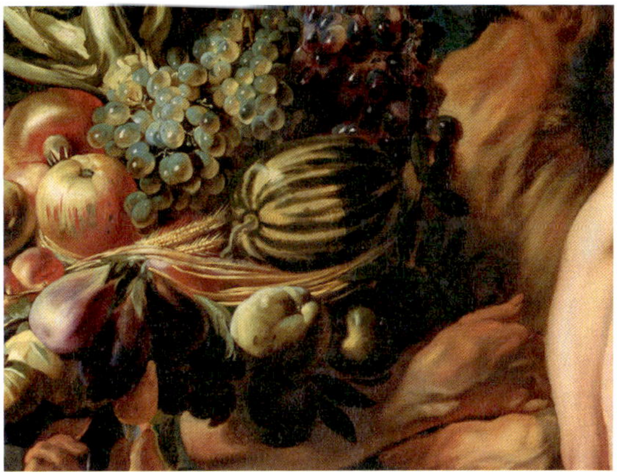

d.

a. Detail of fig. on pp. 6–7

b. Detail of fig. on pp. 6–7

c. Detail of fig. on pp. 6–7

d. Detail of fig. on pp. 6–7

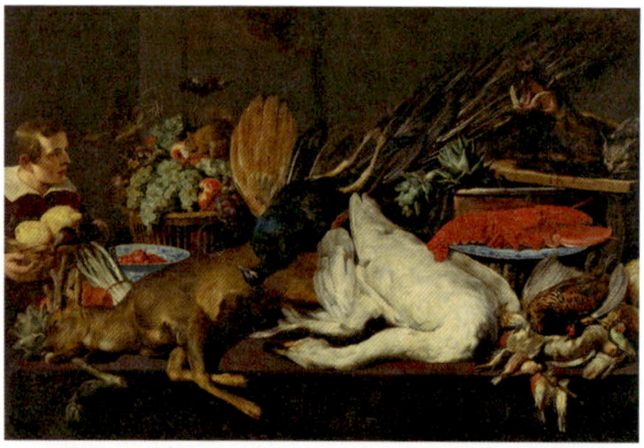

20.

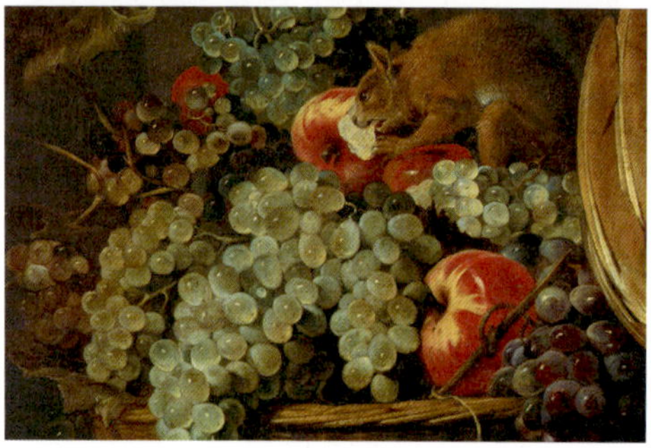

20a.

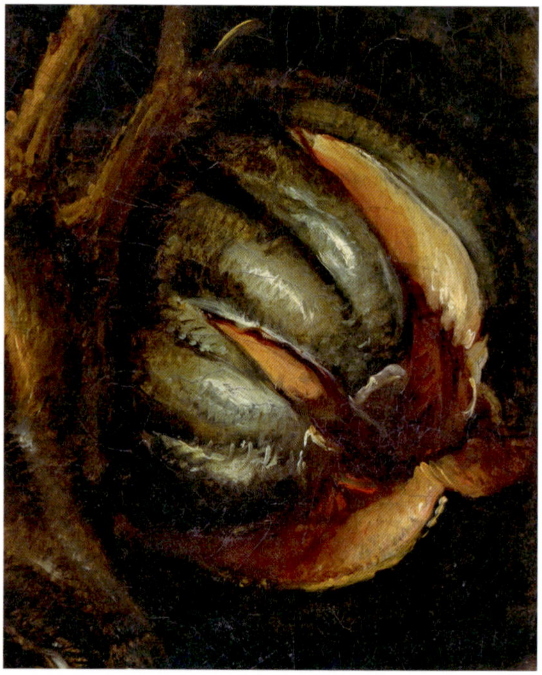

21a.

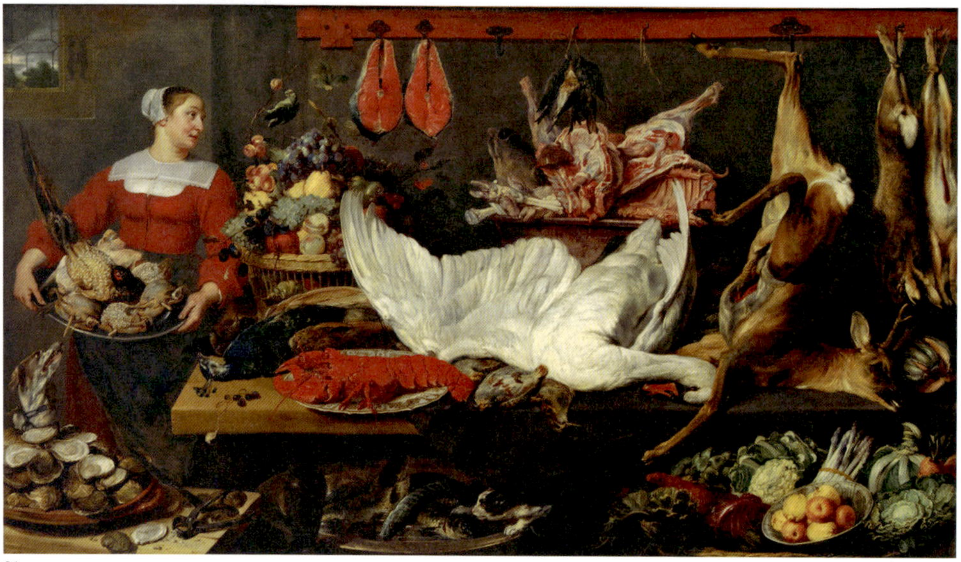

21.

20. Frans Snyders, *Still-life with Swan*, 1616–14, RMFAB, oil on canvas, 145 x 243.5 cm, inv. 187

20a. Detail of fig. 20

21. Frans Snyders and Cornelis de Vos, *The Pantry*, 1630s, RMFAB, oil on canvas, 170 x 290 cm, inv. 3525

21a. Detail of fig. 21

35a. Detail of fig. 35

35b. Detail of fig. 35

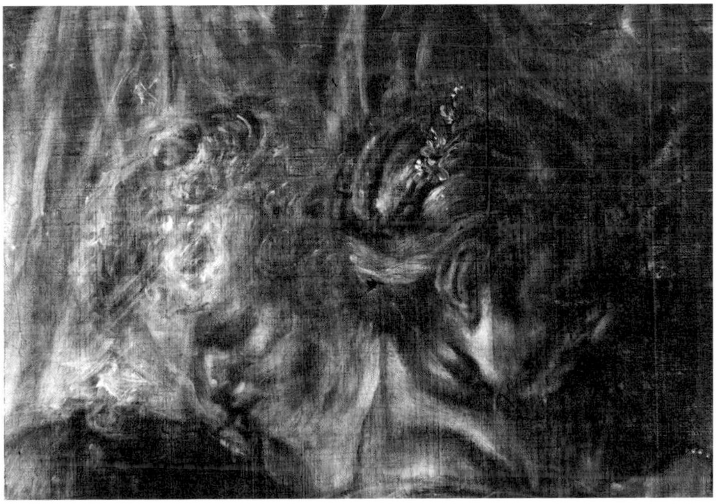

the drawing preceded the paintings in both London and Brussels. The female figure with upraised hand in the background of the Brussels canvas, by contrast, can only be found in the Copenhagen drawing, while the satyr looking at the viewer from the background in the London canvas – which Davis identifies as Silenus[43] – is only found in the Brussels drawing. The second child, a young boy, who looks toward the lower left in the Brussels drawing can be found again in an earlier, overpainted stage of the canvas in the Wallace Collection (fig. 35a), only to change poses once again in the final composition.[44] Last but not least, one of the few pentimenti in the Brussels canvas, in which the red garment of the woman with grapes in her lap has been raised and extended to cover her body (fig. 35b) corresponds fairly closely to the raising of the garment's contour in the Copenhagen sheet with respect to its position in the Brussels sheet. Both drawings seem to have been used for these small yet meaningful alterations to the finished painting in Brussels.

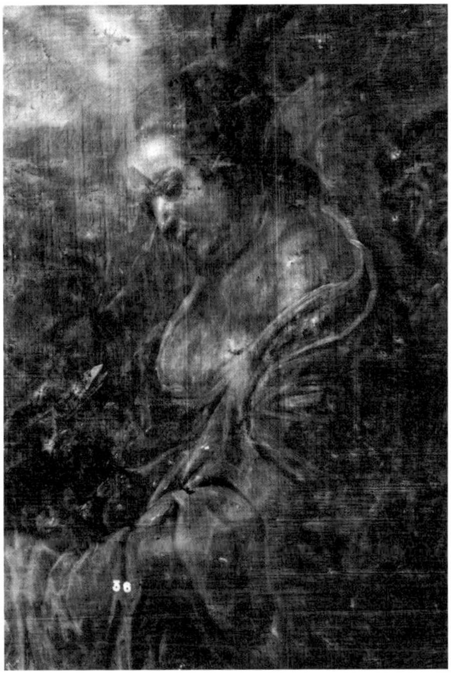

Jordaens was also inspired by antique imagery brought back from Italy by other northern artists. In this respect the reverse of the Brussels drawing deserves more notice than it has received in the past (fig. 22). Although it did not provide any specific motifs for the finished versions of either canvas, its iconography

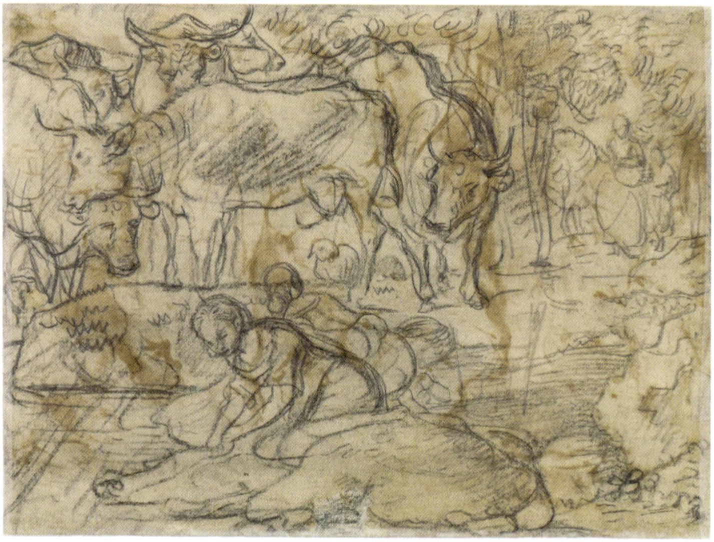

22. Jacques Jordaens, *Allegory of the Land's Fertility* (verso of fig. 14, p. 38), ca. 1623–25, Brussels, RMFAB, pen and brown ink, brown wash, partly over an initial sketch in black chalk, 191 × 261 mm, inv. 6155

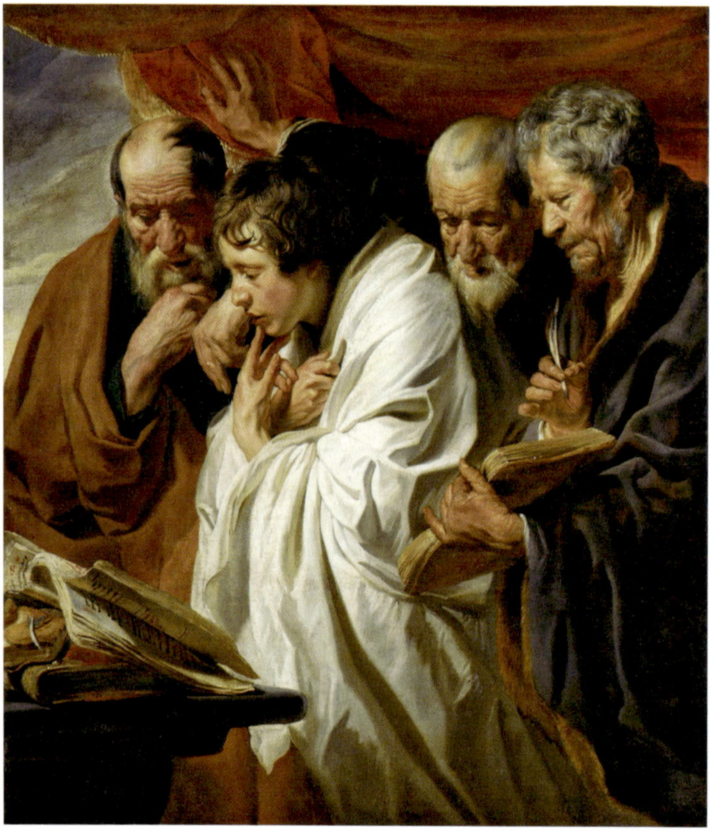

23. Jacques Jordaens, *The Four Evangelists,* ca. 1625–30, Paris, Musée du Louvre, oil on canvas, 134 × 118 cm, inv. 1404

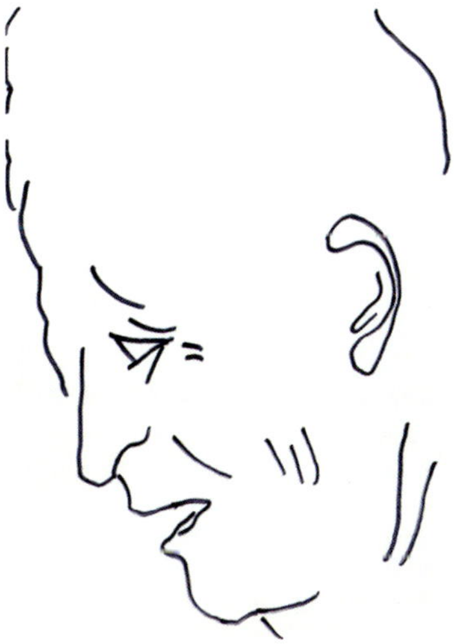

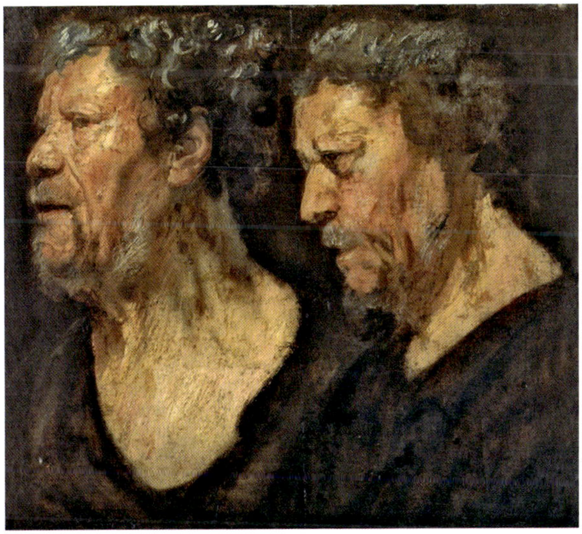

24. Tracing of the head of the evangelist at the right in the Louvre painting (fig. 23) Courtesy of Bruno Mottin

25. Jacques Jordaens, *Two Studies of an Old Man's Head (Abraham Grapheus)*, ca. 1620, Ghent, Museum voor Schone Kunsten, oil on paper, mounted on panel, 45.2 × 52 cm, inv. 1899 B

is indeed relevant in light of the antique subject matter at the heart of both the Brussels and London paintings, as we shall see.[45]

The Use of Head Studies, or "Tronies"

In addition to preparatory drawings, Jordaens also used head studies painted from life in oil on canvas or panel, also known in the seventeenth-century Netherlands as "tronies." Thanks to contour tracings (after an X-ray, fig. 24) made by Bruno Mottin and his colleagues at the Centre de Recherche et de Restauration des Musées de France (C2RMF),[46] we know that the head of the wizened old satyr in the upper right is based on the very same character study that Jordaens used for the evangelist at the far right of his *Four Evangelists* now in the Louvre (fig. 23).[47] Abraham de Graef – also known as Grapheus – served as factotum of the Antwerp Guild of St Luke and was a favorite model among artists of the time, including Jordaens.[48] The study of "tronies" has recently experienced something of a renaissance,[49] and in the case of Grapheus's appearances in Jordaens's oeuvre there has even been an exhibition devoted to the subject in Caen and Ghent.[50] One of the finest examples of such a study, which served as the basis for the heads in the Louvre and Brussels, is now in the permanent collection of the Museum voor Schone Kunsten in Ghent (fig. 25).[51] Although scholars were long aware that this sketch served as the basis for figures in a number of finished paintings by Jordaens,[52] the tracing reveals that their dimensions and contours are almost exactly the same – albeit with functional adjustments to the details. In the Brussels canvas, for example, Grapheus looks toward the three nymphs in the center of the composition, and his ears have been given a point, as befits a satyr, whereas the evangelist in

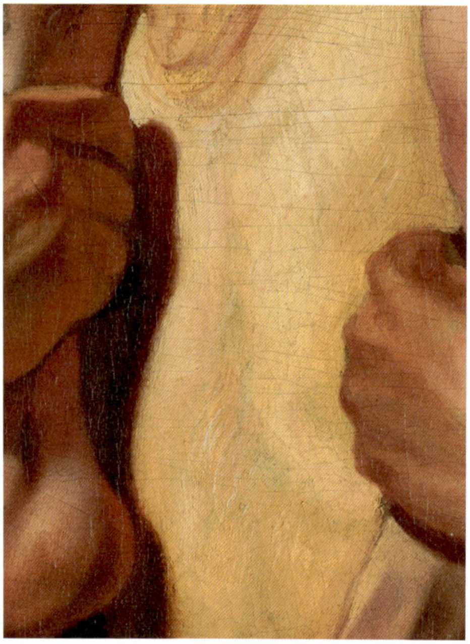

e. Detail of fig. on
pp. 6–7

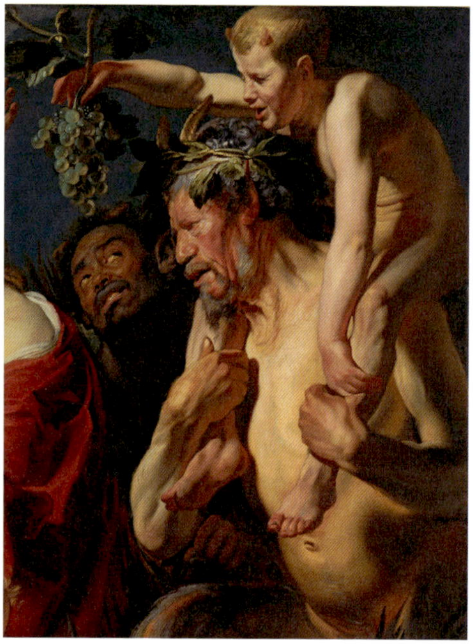

f. Detail of fig. on
pp. 6–7

the Louvre retains his rounded human ears, as one might expect. Although Jordaens used the "earless" head study at the right in the Ghent sketch, he turned to its counterpart at the left for the modeling of Grapheus's ear.[53]

Jordaens incorporated recognizable individuals from his immediate environment into his compositions more frequently than his contemporaries. In the context of genre scenes such as *The King Drinks* and *As the Old Sing, So the Young Pipe,* they contribute to the decorum of the subject according to Cicero's theory of eloquence – after all, comical subjects should be portrayed in a way that is close to nature. Nevertheless, in accordance with Aristotle's notion of mimesis, these figures transcend their naturalistic origins (*imitation vitae*) and become imitation in the true poetic sense (*imago veritas*) because, though lifelike, they are still free creations of the artist's mind.[54] Here, however, we are neither concerned with a genre scene nor a comic representation, but an idealized antique world of demigods, satyrs and nymphs often inspired by sculpture from antiquity. In this context Jordaens's extremely lifelike character heads serve a subtly different function: they answer to a highly specific art-theoretical prescription expressed, among other places, in Rubens's theoretical treatise on the human body, *De Imitatione Statuarum*. Though ancient statues may represents nature idealized, the artist must nevertheless strive to transform the hard stone essence of his models into beings of flesh and blood.[55] In this masterpiece Jordaens succeeds beautifully. The recent restoration, which removed numerous layers of darkened varnish as well as a number of earlier retouches, has revealed these

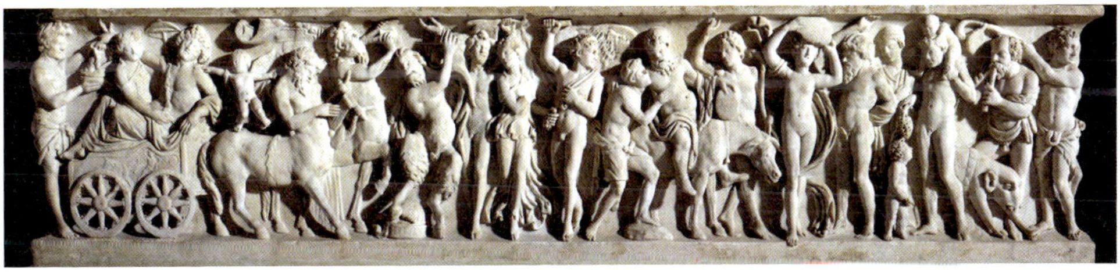

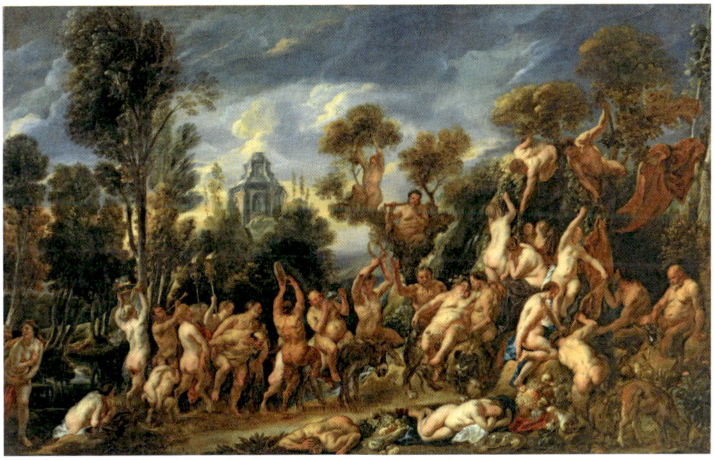

26. Anonymous, Roman Sarcophagus with marriage procession of Bacchus and Ariadne, mid 2nd century AD, London, British Museum, inv. 2298

27. Jacques Jordaens, *The Triumph of Bacchus*, ca. 1645–50, Brussels, RMFAB, oil on canvas, 161 × 260, inv. 3693

beings of flesh and blood even more clearly: in many places the viewer can see not only the difference between smooth, white female skin and rougher, tanned male skin (fig. e), but also the signs of limbs under stress, with tensed muscles and bulging veins (fig. f), about which Rubens discoursed so eloquently in his treatise.[56]

The Use of Antique Visual Sources

One of the most surprising discoveries made during the period of research leading up to the exhibition *Jordaens and the Antique* in 2012–13 was the artist's familiarity with antique sculpture. This conclusion was astonishing, given that there is no documentary proof that Jordaens was ever in Italy. However, the exhibition presented numerous indirect paths by which the artist could have gained insight into the visual culture of antiquity. The paintings in Brussels and London and the associated preparatory drawings in Copenhagen and Brussels must be seen in connection with the treasury of antique visual sources and the specific, purposeful way in which Jordaens put them to use. Jordaens, moreover, used them not only as a source of inspiration for motifs and compositions, but also for iconographic meaning. In all likelihood, Jordaens's interest was sharpened by the considerable number of antique coins and statues in Rubens's art collection in the period between 1619 and 1626 (see essay by Irene Schaudies in this volume).[57]

One of the most important sources for Jordaens's inventions in Brussels and London – formally and iconographically – was a well-known Roman sarcophagus from the 2nd

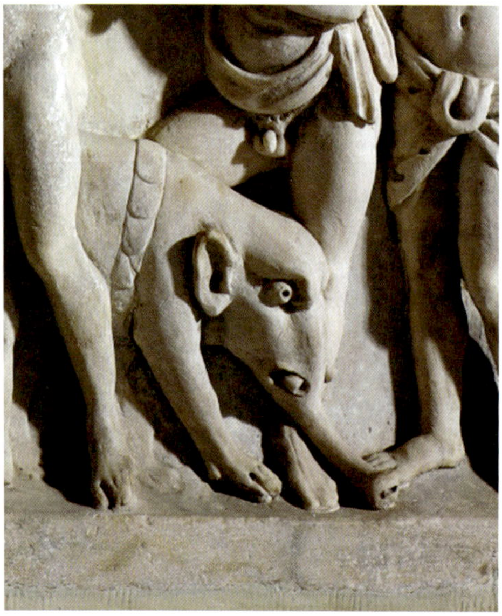

26a. Detail of fig. 26

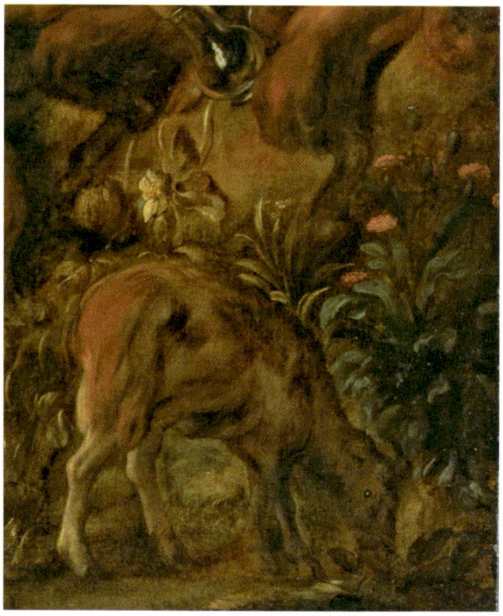

27a. Detail of fig. 27

century AD, now held in the British Museum (fig. 26).[58] Reproduced in an engraving by Battista Franco (ca. 1530–61), the sarcophagus would have been familiar to artists and connoisseurs alike.[59] Jordaens may also have had access to drawings by Rubens – whose archeological passion for antiquity is well known[60] – or Abraham Janssen,[61] who, like Rubens, had also spent several years in Rome, though no such study by either painter survives. Lacunae in the relief were filled in during the sixteenth century at the pope's expense.[62] But Jordaens does not distinguish between figures added later and the antique originals, let alone between more and less questionable additions. For example, he borrows freely the figure of a child that was added later, and in a later painting, the *Triumph of Bacchus,* now in Brussels (fig. 27), he would transform a clumsy later addition to a fragmentary antique animal, which vaguely resembles an elephant (fig. 26a), into a peculiar chimera that seems to be half goat, half cow (fig. 27a). Although it is clear that Jordaens's interest was not primarily archeological, he must nevertheless have seen antique artworks as normative: as models to imitate, equal, and even surpass.[63] He also had an eye for decorum. The old satyr carrying a young boy on his back at the far right in the Brussels and London canvases was taken over directly from the sarcophagus (fig. 26b). But in the finished paintings, the ithyphallic satyr of the sarcophagus no longer displays his arousal; instead, only his upper body is visible – a shift that can also be seen in the Brussels drawing. In the Brussels canvas a nymph has replaced him, but in both cases the upraised arms of Bacchus's ithyphallic companion have been cited literally. The overall erotic charge is suggested rather than explicitly displayed by the gesture of the young girl who pulls away the reeds from before the satyr's genitals in both paintings – genitals that are not clearly visible

26b. Detail of fig. 26

28. Anonymous, *Venus Kallipygos*, 1st or 2nd century BC, Naples, Museo Archeologico Nazionale, inv. 6020

29. Anonymous, Female figure known as the *Shell Nymph*, 1st century BC, Paris, Musée du Louvre, inv. MR 309, MA18

30. Anonymous, Roman copy, *Crouching Venus*, (Knidos type), 2nd century, London, Collection of Her Majesty the Queen, on loan to the British Museum, By Gracious Permission of H.M. the Queen, reg. no. 1963.1029.1

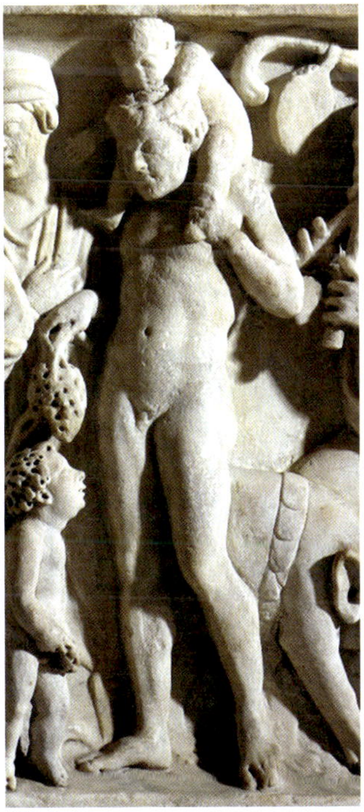

26b.

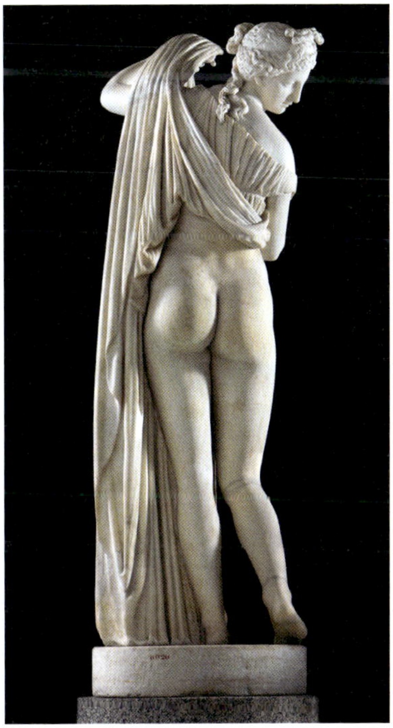

28.

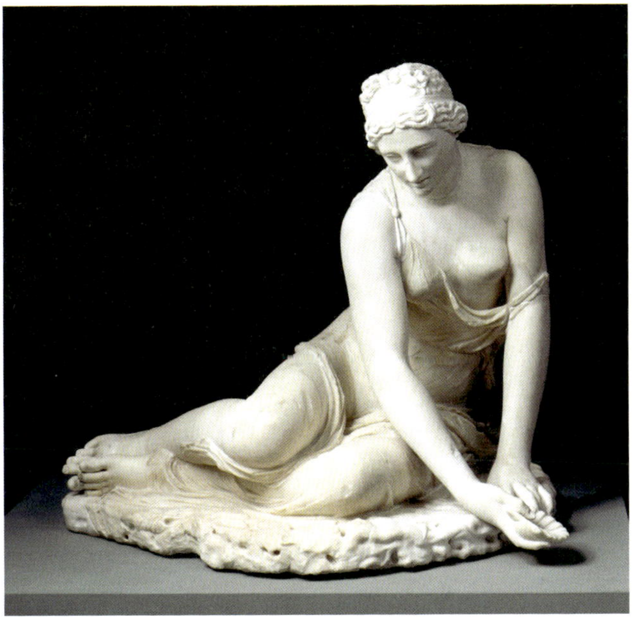

29.

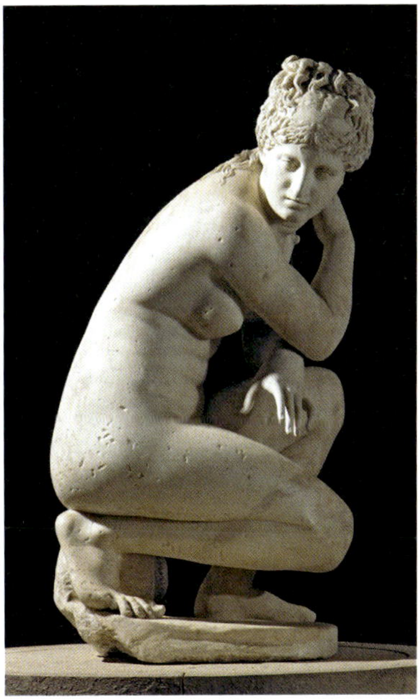

30.

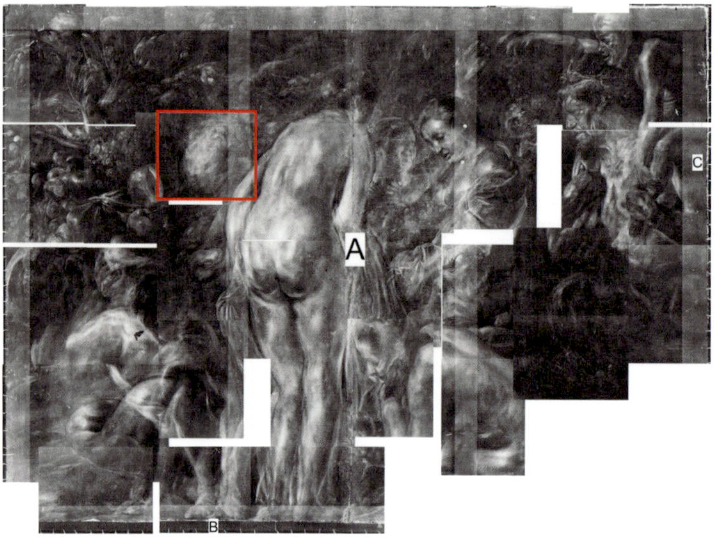

31. Radiograph mosaic of inv. 119 (fig., pp. 6–7)

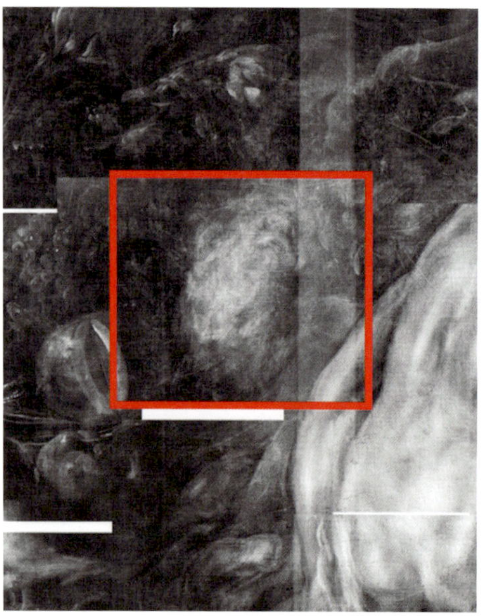

31a. Detail of fig. 31

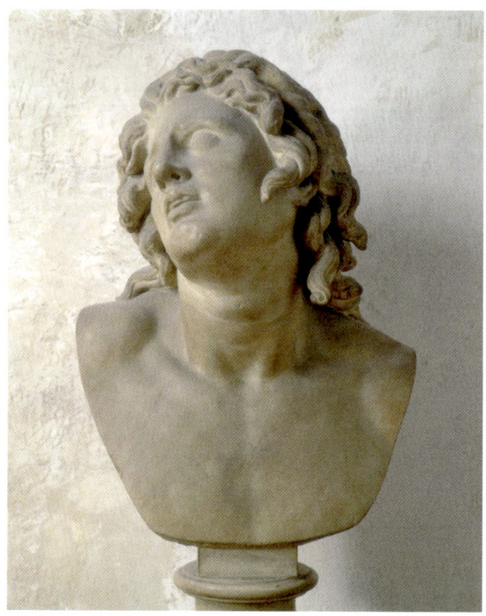

32. Anonymous, *Dying Alexander*, 3rd / 2nd century BC, Florence, Galleria degli Uffizi, inv. 338

in either the drawn or painted compositions. Both drawings still show Silenus's donkey, also found on the sarcophagus: at the right in the Brussels sheet; and at the left, but almost entirely cut off, in the Copenhagen sheet. In both sheets Jordaens varies the different heads to the left of the satyr carrying the child.

Here too he experiments quite explicitly with antique sources for the central figure in both paintings. In the Brussels canvas he chooses a magnificent figure seen from behind, based on the renowned antique statue of the *Venus Kallipygos* (fig. 28),[64] or Venus with the beautiful buttocks.[65] For the crouching satyr at the left, Jordaens combines the poses of two different satyrs on the sarcophagus – one with upraised arms and one that crouches – with that of the famed *Venus of Knidos* (fig. 30), though in the Brussels drawing this figure is still closer to the version on the sarcophagus. This fusion is *pièce de résistance* that does not stop at the slavish copying (*transposition*) of antique models, but rather takes imitation (*imitatio*) to the level of emulation (*aemulatio*), or an attempt to surpass them.[66] The pensive nymph seated in the foreground is based on a similarly famous model, the *Nymph with a Shell* (fig. 29), a Roman statue from the 2nd century AD now in the Louvre. Her pose gradually evolves in the drawings in Copenhagen and Brussels, illustrating once again the workings of Jordaens's creative process in visual terms.

The Painting's Coherence and the Artist's Confidence

The highly uniform genesis of the pictorial layers, with only minor adjustments to the composition, as shown in the X-rays (fig. 31),[67] stands in stark contrast to the turbulent, long-term genesis of the London canvas. This is a strong argument in favor of the position taken by Lucy Davis (see her essay in this volume), that the Brussels canvas was created over a short period of time before leaving the workshop soon afterward. The striking uniformity moreover suggests that this quickly executed canvas was probably made with a specific patron in mind. The iconographic nuances that Jordaens incorporated into the painting also point in this direction when compared to his other compositions with the same theme.

One of the few changes that Jordaens made to the Brussels canvas – in contrast to the several phases of overpainting that characterize its London counterpart – was to paint out the head of a satyr based on an antique model, the *Dying Alexander* (fig. 32), which is still visible in the X-ray under the spreading abundance of the cornucopia (fig. 31a). The elimination of this well-known Pathosformule represents a relative decrease in antique sources. In addition, the head of the young boy seated on the satyr's shoulders at the right was also raised – perhaps because it, too, like the head of the satyr, was based on a "tronie." To the left of this pair, there was originally a head looking downward that has been replaced by the head of a black man looking upward. A head in the original pose appears on the sarcophagus that served Jordaens as a model for the overall composition as well as in the Brussels drawing (fig. 14, p. 38). Its presence in the latter forms additional proof of the role played by the drawings in the creation of the Brussels canvas.

In addition, thread-count analysis (see essay by Don Johnson) reveals that the canvas was probably cut down slightly on the left side (perhaps eliminating Silenus's mount?), but not above or below. The restoration moreover confirmed d'Hulst's 1952 observation that all four edges were trimmed during relining – also above, near the top of the little boy's head – and a narrow strip of different canvas was added below (see report by Pham Thanh-Nghi). D'Hulst's presumption of a substantial reduction of the Brussels canvas above, however, which was based on the more vertical compositional field of the drawing and the London painting, does not find support in Johnson's results.[68] It also appears that the relining canvas and the current stretcher frame are unusually old. According to radiocarbon analysis conducted under the auspices of the University of Aarhus, the relining most likely dates to ca. 1740[69] – a hypothesis that is not contradicted by additional analyses of the relining canvas, carried out under the supervision of Jørgen

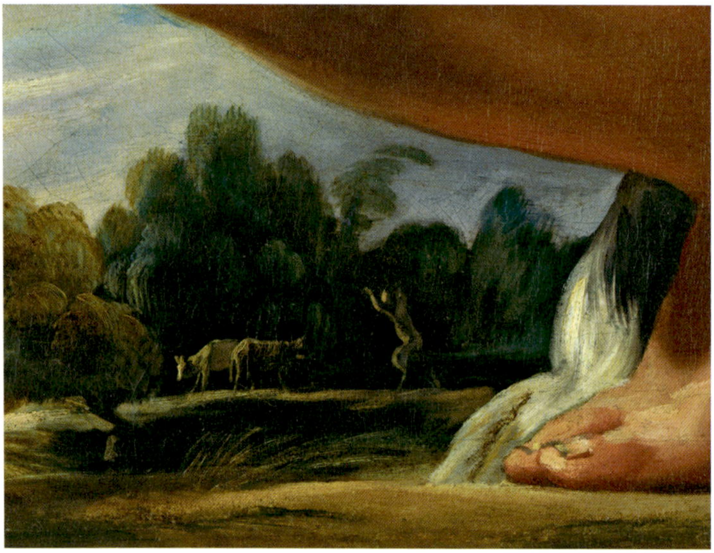

g. Detail of figure pp. 6–7

Wadum,[70] and samples of the adhesive, conducted by Steven Saverwyns.[71] The results of the various technical investigations are further supported by what is known of the painting's early provenance.[72] Based on these findings, the international commission charged with advising the museum on the restoration decided not to replace the stretcher frame, which was beginning to split in places, but rather to stabilize it. The relining was also left untouched, in spite of the fact that it caused the vertical seam of the original canvas to produce an unsightly relief, and resulted in distortion of the lower left-hand corner of the painting (see the report by Pham Thanh-Nghi).

The Relationship between Pictorial Logic and Patron

As noted in the introductory essay to this volume, the paintings in Brussels and London belong to a larger group of related pictures, all of which deal with fertility and abundance. In the exhibition catalogue *Jordaens and the Antique,* I have tried to show how Jordaens's exploration of these themes is related to the ancient notion of Peace, and that many artworks in this group were, not coincidentally, painted in periods when the expectation of peace – or fear of war – was particularly intense.[73] Irene Schaudies has moreover pointed to the relevant iconographical variation in Jordaens's choice of antique sources, textual and otherwise. Jordaens did not employ these sources crudely or at random, as has often been believed – particularly in comparison to Rubens.[74] This sense of iconographic nuance translates, in the case of Jordaens, into the choice of differing motifs from one version to another within the thematic group – a choice that is by no means arbitrary. The motifs used by Jordaens possess an emblematic character that allows them to give a specific moralizing commentary on antique narrative. The provenance of the Brussels canvas points in the direction of the deliberate orientation of the iconography towards a specific patron or purchaser.

In Ovid's account of the cornucopia's origin, the naiads, or water nymphs fill the horn of Achelous, which had been broken off in combat

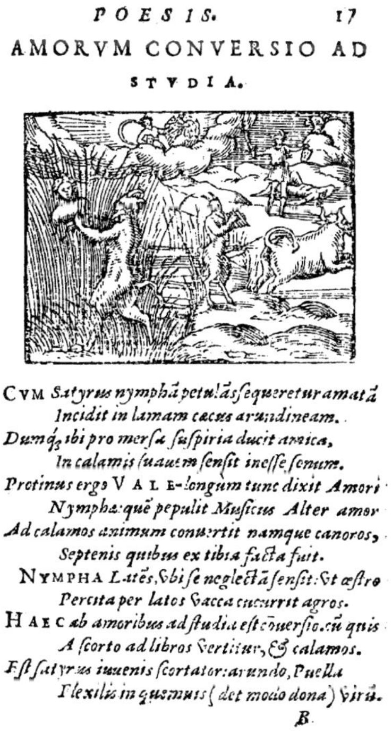
POESIS. 17
AMORVM CONVERSIO AD STVDIA.

CVM Satyrus nympham petulas ſequeretur amatā
Incidit in lamam caecus arundineam.
Dumq; ibi pro merſa ſuſpiria ducit amica,
In calamis ſuauem ſenſit ineſſe ſonum.
Protinus ergo VALE longum tunc dixit Amori
Nymphaeque pepulit Muſicus Alter amor
Ad calamos animum conuertit namque canoros,
Septenis quibus ex tibia facta fuit.
NYMPHA Latēs, Vbi ſe neglectā ſenſit: Vt aeſtro
Percita per latos Vacca cucurrit agros.
HAEC ab amoribus ad ſtudia eſt cōuerſio. cū quis
A ſcorto ad libros Vertitur, & calamos.
Eſt ſatyrus iuuenis ſcortator: arundo, Puella
Flexilis in quemuis (det modo dona) Virū.
B.

33. Amorum Conversio Ad Studia, emblem in H. Barthélemy, *Picta poesis*, Lyon, 1552

by Hercules. In the Munich *Allegory of Fertility* of ca. 1616–17 the naiads are clearly visible at the lower left, and their presence is entirely in accordance with Ovid's text (fig. 44, p. 24, detail lower left). But in the Brussels canvas, only the barest hint of water remains; the nymphs in the lower-left corner have been omitted, and only a satyr chasing a lone cow remains (fig. g). A similar cow appears in the same place on the London canvas, under the current paint layer, though it is invisible on the X-ray.

It is no coincidence that cows happen to be one of Jordaens's favorite motifs. In the antique doctrine of the Four Elements, they refer not to Water – in accord with the origin myth of the cornucopia – but to the element Earth as pointed out by Joaneath Spicer.[75] Perhaps not surprisingly, the reverse of the Brussels preparatory drawing for the *Allegory of Fertility* features a group of milkmaids and cows (fig. 22, p. 54, verso of fig. 14, p. 38): another theme which refers, albeit indirectly, to the fertility of the Earth. In her study of the origins of the Dutch cattle piece, Spicer uncovered the close allegorical associations between cows, abundance, wealth and property, the fertility of the earth and of women. Such associations are made explicitly in the legends of engravings after Willem Buytewech (1591–1624), with cattle motifs used to illustrate themes such as the element Earth or the season spring. Moreover, those legends date from around the same time as Jordaens's painting in Brussels. Raising cattle was not only an important aspect of agriculture in the seventeenth century, but also one of the four aspects of country life that Virgil explicitly discusses in his *Georgics*.[76] As Matías Díaz Padrón has remarked, the spirit of the *Georgics* permeates Rubens's many paintings of country life featuring cows and milkmaids.[77] Indeed, around 1621, shortly before Jordaens painted his Brussels allegory, cows and milkmaids also played a prominent role in many landscapes and drawings by Rubens, and in a much more explicit way than in his great predecessor in landscape, Pieter Bruegel the Elder. Jan Brueghel the Elder moreover cites many of Rubens's rural motifs directly in scenes that explicitly deal with the fruitfulness of life on the land, such as the *Flemish Dairy* now in the Prado.[78] Moreover, the motif of a satyr or satyrs chasing a cow was not chosen at random: it goes back to a well-known French emblem book (fig. 33), which in its commentary suggests that one follow the satyr's example, and exchange the instincts of nature for study and culture (that is, the idea of agriculture as a counterpart to the pure, undiluted drives of Nature in its untamed

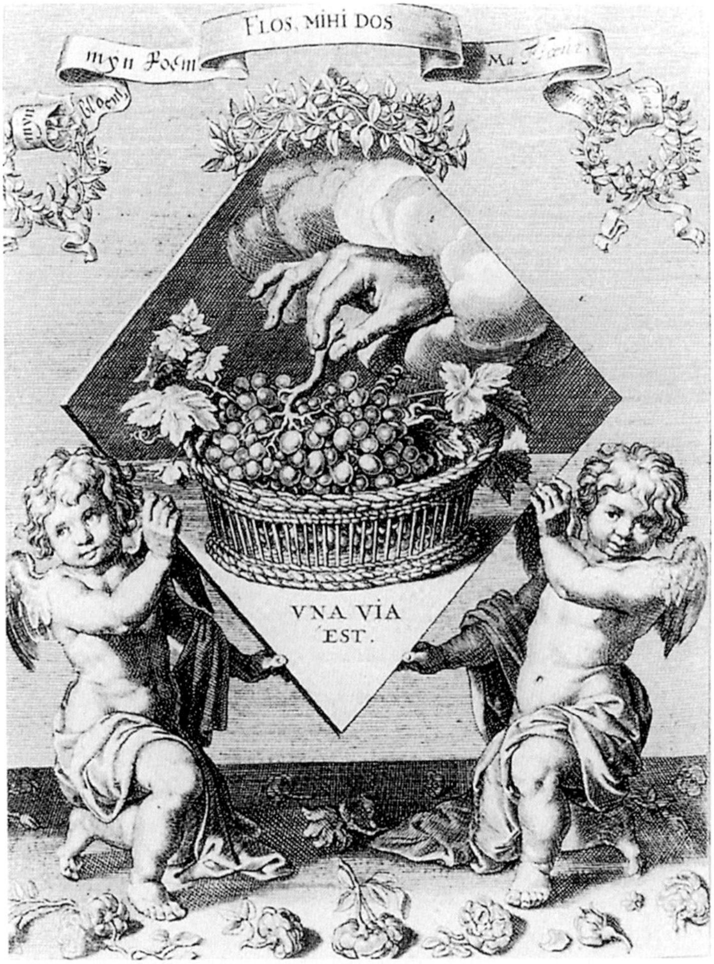

34. J. Swelinck (?) after Adriaen van de Venne, *Collection of Emblems Dedicated to All Chaste Maidens*, in Jacob Cats, Maechden-plicht, Middelburg, 1618

state).[79] This warning against allowing the natural instincts to get the upper hand is also present in the motif of the seated nymph, who carefully holds a cluster of grapes by the stem, without touching the fruit itself.[80] Grapes may be associated with bacchic ecstasy, but in emblem books the deliberate preservation of the grapes symbolizes the deliberate preservation of a woman's virginity before marriage (fig. 34).[81]

The earliest known provenance of the Brussels canvas leads back to the Della Faille, a well-known family of highly educated, wealthy merchants who at the end of the sixteenth century were elevated to the nobility, after which they became bankers and landowners of considerable stature.[82] The branch of the family in The Hague that once owned the Brussels painting was undoubtedly from Southern Netherlandish descent.[83] It is not likely that they acquired the picture from Jordaens's descendants, because the Della Faille's painting was sold at auction in 1730,[84] four years before the sale of artworks from the Jordaens estate.[85] Moreover, the Della Failles had been acquiring artworks since they were ennobled,[86] and they continued to commission altarpieces in both Ghent and Antwerp throughout the 1620s – i.e. the period when Jordaens's painting was created – from renowned history painters such as Rubens, Van Dyck, Abraham Janssen, and Jan Janssens.[87] While there is no definitive evidence that they commissioned the Brussels allegory from Jordaens, its provenance and their pedigree – as well as their status as prominent patrons of the arts in the seventeenth century – makes them highly probable candidates. They had every reason to appreciate the prestigious format of a large, costly history painting with an elevated antique theme. The iconographic accents of the Brussels canvas would probably have been to their taste. The theme of peace was near and dear to the hearts of bankers and merchants, as peace was the best guarantee of thriving trade, a flourishing economy, and robust financial system – preferably without bankrupt princes who could not pay their troops and devalued their currency. The accent placed on the Earth and its abundant fertility must also have appealed to the owners of extensive property.[88] And for a noble dynasty that needed to strengthen its patrimony through prudent marriage politics, and hoped to improve its chances on the marriage market through a good education, the moralizing lessons of an honorable marriage and the choice of study and culture above the untrammeled instincts of nature were undoubtedly worthy of embracing.

By Way of Conclusion

A multidisciplinary analysis of the genesis of *Allegory of Fertility* in Brussels and the *Allegory of Fruitfulness* in London, in cooperation with professors, curators, and restorers has lead to innovative and unexpected conclusions concerning the chronological, technical, and artistic relationship between the two works. Jordaens's role in both cases appears to have been even greater than previously thought, without the aid of horizontal (Snyders) or vertical (apprentices) collaboration. Jordaens appears all the more to be a master whose use of antique narrative and visual sources is thoughtful and nuanced. Jordaens was a painter who radically revised his compositions while painting, yet he was also customer oriented, adapting his artistic and commercial logic as the situation demanded.

[1] An explanation of this title can be found in Vander Auwera, 2007-2008, pp. 165–69. In contrast to the French distinction between human fertility (*fécondité*) and the fertility of nature (*fertilité*), English "fertility" encompasses both. This corresponds more closely to the double meaning of the Latin word *ubertas*. Jordaens's allegory goes back to this dual antique concept. The emblematic scene in the lower left background emphasizes the ancient element Earth (see below).

[2] The museum only became a national institution in 1843. For this reason, documents concerning the purchase are found in the Brusselse Stadsarchief, Bestand van het Openbaar Onderwijs, 1ste reeks, 106, folios 289–91. See Van Kalck et al. 2003, I, p. 121, n. 77.

[3] Inv. 120, oil on canvas, 120 × 117 cm. Compositional sketch for one of the most prominent, monumental canvases decorating the Oranjezaal in Huis ten Bosch near The Hague, memorializing this prince at the request of his widow Amalia van Solms. Purchased by the curator Bosschaert as "une grande esquisse de Jaq: Jordaens representant l'entrée triomphante du Prince d'orange à Lahaije" for 638 French francs on August 25, 1806, at the request of the mayor of Brussels. Archief van de Stad Brussel, Finance, Livre des catégoris de 1809, p. 97, and Grand livre des recettes et dépenses, 9, 1809.

[4] The Dutch version, *Inventariscatalogus van de oude schilderkunst, Koninklijke Musea voor Schone Kunsten van België, Departement Oude Kunst* (Brussels, 1984), p. 156, erroneously lists 1927 as the purchase date, probably thanks to a typographical mistake. Its French counterpart, *Catalogue inventaire de la peinture ancienne, Musées royaux des Beaux-Arts de Belgique, Département d'Art Ancien* (Brussels, 1984), p. 156, gives the correct date. See Van Kalck et al. 2003, I, p. 121.

[5] Inv. 121, oil on canvas, 59 × 48 cm. Catalogued for the first time in 1806.

[6] Inv. 118, oil on canvas, 432 × 269 cm; signed and dated *1630*.

[7] For the power struggle between Paris and Brussels in connection with the return of the paintings, see Van Kalck et al. 2003, I, pp. 45–78.

[8] Peter Carpreaux, "The 'Nachleben' of Jacob Jordaens, (1593-1678): An Inquiry, Based on Auction Prices," in Münch/Pataki 2012, pp. 465–81, esp. p. 471*ff.*

[9] Génard 1852, p. 231, nro 45. Mentioned in a typed note in the museum files.

[10] Rooses 1906, pp. 45–47.

[11] Buschmann 1905, pp. 77–80.

[12] *Exposition de l'Art Belge Ancien et Moderne*, Paris, Musée du Jeu de Paume, 10 May–10 July1923, cat. 41.

[13] *Rubens et son temps*, Paris, Musée de l'Orangerie, 1936, pp. 76, 78, cat. 42.

[14] *Van Jan van Eyck tot Rubens: Tentoonstelling van Meesterwerken uit Belgische musea en kerken*, Amsterdam, Rijksmuseum, 25 March–19 May 1946; Rotterdam, Museum Boymans, 25 May–16 June 1946, p. 30, cat. 39.

[15] *Exposition d'oeuvres de Jordaens et de son atelier. Musées royaux des Beaux-arts de Belgique*, Brussels, 27 October–12 November 1928, cat. 80. Organized by recently appointed curator Leo Van Puyvelde, who was interested in Jordaens and in 1953 wrote a monograph on the artist (see also note 35).

[16] See Van Kalck et al. 2003, II, p. 727.

[17] *Chefs d'Oeuvre de l'Art Ancien dans les Musées et Collections Belges / Meesterwerken van Oude Kunst uit Belgische Musea en Verzamelingen*, Brussels, Palais des Beaux-Arts, exhibition in honor of the institution's 25th anniversary, 1953, cat. 49.

[18] Brussels/Kassel 2012–13.

[19] As indicated by the titles of the exhibitions mentioned in notes 12 and 14.

[20] D'Hulst 1952, pp. 18–31.

[21] This is clear from internal evidence in the museum files. The preparatory restoration report itself, however, drawn up by Albert Philippot onf December 22, 1966, can no longer be found in the museum file in which it was originally kept, nor does KIK/IRPA have a duplicate.

[22] KMSKB/MRBAB, Archief Zaalopnamen/Vue des salles, "Musée d'art ancien, salles avant transformations, 01.02.1974, [photo nos.] 111395>111428 M, Salle X (Rubens et Jordaens), [photo no.] 111424" [from KIK/IRPA].

[23] *Ibid.*, [photo nos.] 17708 N > 17767 N, [photo no.] 17750 N [from KIK/IRPA], "Balat Museum, Zaal 57 – Jordaens, januari 1999."

[24] This idea of Edmond Ritter's, published in *Flandre au Lion* (1958), was recently cited by Ludo Beheydt in *Eén en toch apart: Kunst en cultuur in de Nederlanden* (Leuven-Zwolle, 2002), p. 195, in which Jordaens's commissions for the court of the Dutch stadholder were once again indicated as representatives of Dutch national feeling and as proof of cultural unity between the North and South Netherlands.

[25] Münch/Pataki 2012.

[26] Brussels, KMSKB/MRBAB, 6–7 December 2012, and Kassel, Museumslandschaft Hessen Kassel, Orangerie, 5–6 May 2013 (a shared publication is being prepared).

[27] Of the Statens Museum for Kunst and the Universiteit van Amsterdam. The other members were: Livia Depuydt-Elbaum (Koninklijk Instituut voor het Kunstpatrimonium, Brussel); Irene Schaudies, (IUAP, Royal Museums of Fine Arts of Belgium, Brussels); Michel van de Laar (Rijksmuseum Amsterdam); Joost Vander Auwera (Royal Museums of Fine Arts of Belgium, Brussels); Nico Van Hout (Koninklijk Museum voor Schone Kunsten Antwerpen), and Jos Van Och (Stichting Restauratie Atelier Limburg, Maastricht).

[28] See Peeters 2007, the results of a workshop on journeyman painterss held at the Rijksuniversiteit Groningen on 23–24 May 2003.

[29] One of the objectives of the workshop at the Universiteit Groningen (see n. 28) was to make visible workshop assistants who usually remained "under the radar" by means of various archival sources. That guild registers such as the well-known Antwerp *Liggeren* only provide an official, "sanitized" version of reality is also evident from my discovery of and comparison to the unofficial calculations of dean Abraham I Janssen (Liège? Ca. 1571/75–Antwerp 1632) in the context of my dissertation on the painter. See Vander Auwera 2003.
[30] D'Hulst 1952, p. 20, proposes this date on the basis of stylistic similarities to the *Homage to Ceres* in Madrid (IS_6) and the *Tribute Money* now in Copenhagen (Statens Museum for Kunst, inv. KMS3198). It was originally dated somewhat later (1625–28) by Rooses (Rooses 1906, p. 46). Recent research has shown that the history and dating of the Copenhagen canvas is much complexer that previously believed: it was probably begun around 1623 and expanded by the master in various stages, perhaps even as late as the 1660s. See Copenhagen 2008.
[31] See the chronology drawn up by R.-A. d'Hulst and Nora De Poorter in Antwerp 1993, I, p. 7.
[32] *Idem.*, p. 8.
[33] *Ibid.*
[34] See the introductory remarks of N. Peeters and J. Dambruyne in Peeters 2007, p. xv, n. 37: "This [i.e. the average of four years training] was an article in the statutes of some artists' corporations, but was often variable."
[35] Rooses 1906 only mentions Jordaens as author of the work, as does R.-A. d'Hulst in Antwerp 1993, I, p. 48 (sub. ill. A4b) and p. 96 (sub. ill. A21a), and II, p. 12 (sub. ill. B6a) and p. 20 (sub. ill. B10a). Arnout Balis does not see Snyders' hand in the picture at all. Snyders specialists Hella Robels (Robels 1989) and Susan Koslow (Koslow 1995) do not discuss the Brussels picture at all. However, the issue is discussed in the aforementioned exhibition catalogues of 1928, cat. 80 (cfr. supra, n. 15); 1936, cat. 42, pp. 76–77 (cfr. supra, n. 13); 1946, p. 30, cat. 39 (cfr. supra, n. 14), and 1953, cat. 49 (cfr. supra, n. 17). The attribution of still-life elements to Snyders was also supported by Albert Dasnoy in the popular edition of the *Fondation Cultura* 2/35 of 1965 and by Leo van Puyvelde in *Le siècle de Rubens/de eeuw van Rubens*, exh. cat. Bruxelles/Brussel, MRBAB/KMSKB, 1965, cat. 126. Van Puyvelde would adhere to the dual attribution to Jordaens and Snyders until the end of his life. John C. Van Dyke, *Brussels, Antwerp: critical notes on the royal Museums at Brussels and Antwerp* (New York, 1914), pp. 31–32, attributes the fruit to Snyders and deems it "rubbish lugged in to fill up and might better have been left out. It was lugged in by Snyders, not Jordaens." He considered the version in the Wallace Collection "a variation" on the Brussels canvas. Minna Heimbürger, "About an Unsolved Jacob Jordaens Problem," *Konsthistorisk Tidskrift* 64 (1995), pp. 215–39, esp. pp. 225, 227 (fig. 7), and 228, was one of the last defenders of the idea that Snyders had a part in the picture, although retouched by Jordaens. My predecessor Willy Laureyssens (Laureyssens 1993), p. 46, was also convinced of Snyders' coauthorship, as I was in *Musée d'Art Ancien, Oeuvres choisies* (Brussels, 2001), p. 142. One still finds echoes of this opinion outside art history proper; for example, in Axel Kahn and Yvan Brohard, *Les âges de la vie: Mythes, arts, sciences* (Paris, 2012).
[36] *Diana's Return from the Hunt,* in Dresden (Staatliche Kunstsammlungen, Gemäldegalerie, inv. 962A, oil on canvas, 136 × 184 cm) and Darmstadt (Hessisches Landesmuseum, inv. GK 180, oil on canvas, 231 × 278 cm), respectively. Both date to ca. 1615 and are illustrated in Koslow 1995, p. 240, figs. 324–25.
[37] The influence of Rubens was quickly noted: Rooses 1906 already mentions it, pp. 45–46.
[38] RMFAB, inv. 187: *Still-life with Swan*; inv. 3229: *Stag Hunt*; inv. 3525: *The Pantry*; inv. 3361, *Still-life with Fish and Crustaceans*, shows traces of a signature.
[39] This difference, quite distinct when inspecting the paintings themselves, is even visible in reproduction.
[40] D'Hulst 1974, I, cat. A64, pp. 157–58 (III, fig. 73), and cat. A63, pp. 156–57 (III, fig. 72).
[41] The size of which is more or less original (see essay by Anna Sandén).
[42] The watermark is closest to that of a French paper mill (Briquet no. 8074). My thanks to Stefaan Hautekeete of the Drawing Cabinet of the RMFAB for rechecking the watermark.
[43] This identification is supported by the presence of a figure with a similar physiognomy and pose on the Roman sarcophagus that inspired Jordaens (see below). There, he is seated on a donkey, the traditional attribute of Silenus.
[44] The iconographic relevance of this reference and its Rubensian tint, also noted by Lucy Davis, may be related to its possible patron; see below.
[45] R.-A. d'Hulst (D'Hulst 1952, p. 30, and ill. 8, pp. 29–30, and Antwerp 1993, II, p. 20, cat. B10) rightly refers to its greater kinship with a drawing entitled *Diana and Callisto,* now in the Städelsches Kunstinstitut in Frankfurt (inv. 5867, pen, brush, brown ink, 149 x 212 mm), which W. Drost, "Motivenübername bei Jacob Jordaens und Adriaen Brouwer," *Königsberger Kunstgeschichtliche Forschungen* 1 (1928), p. 12, attributes to Adam Elsheimer; H. Möhle, *Die Zeichnungen von Adam Elsheimer* (Berlin, 1966), pp. 77–78, and Jan G. van Gelder and Ingrid Jost, "Elsheimers unverteilter Nachlass, II," *Simiolus* 2 (1967–68), p. 27, attribute it to Hendrik Goudt (for an overview of the attributions see Joachim Jacoby, *Die Zeichnungen von Adam Elsheimer: Kritischer Katalog* (Frankfurt, 2008), p. 357 (in Konkordanz B).
[46] Written communication, 9 April 2008 and 24 April 2008 (both in the museum files). My thanks to Mr. Mottin for allowing us to publish these tracings.
[47] Inv. 1404, oil on canvas, 134 × 118 cm.

[48] See Antwerp 1993, I, cat. 121, pp. 96–97, with a summary of earlier literature on the subject.
[49] See the *International Symposium accompanying the Exhibition "Tronies - Marlene Dumas and the Old Masters,* Munich, Haus der Kunst, 29 October 2010–6 February 2011. For the program see: http://www.codart.nl/exhibitions/details/2244/ (accessed 1 April 2014).
[50] See Nico Van Hout, "Les tronies: L'emploi des têtes de caractère dans la peinture d'histoire flamande," in Caroline Joubert et al. *Jacob Jordaens et son modèle Abraham Grapheus,* exh. cat. Caen (Musée des Beaux-Arts de Caen) / Ghent (Museum voor Schone Kunsten), 2012, pp. 35–43.
[51] Museum voor Schone Kunsten, inv. 1899 B, oil on paper, mounted on panel, 45,2 × 52 cm.
[52] Compare Antwerp 1993, I, cat. A 21.
[53] A sketch of a Grapheus-like head sold as a Jordaens (Christie's, London, 31 March 1989, lot 109), also shows the right hand in the same position as in the Brussels painting, a hand that is missing on the Roman sarcophagus.
[54] Irene Schaudies, "Jordaens, le bourgeois absolu?" in Paris 2013, pp. 58–59.
[55] See Jeffrey Muller's magisterial article, "Rubens's Theory and Practice of the Imitation of Art," *Art Bulletin* 64 (1982), pp. 229–47.
[56] In his theoretical notebook on the human figure, Rubens points out that the places on the human body where the muscles are regularly worked receive better circulation of the blood.
[57] Irene Schaudies, "Antiquity and its Uses," Brussels/Kassel 2013–13, p. 77.
[58] A.H. Smith, *A Catalogue of Sculpture in the Department of Greek and Roman Antiquities, British Museum,* III (London, 1904), pp. 301–04, no. 2298. F. Matz, *Die dionysischen Sarcophage,* II, *Die antiken Sarkophagereliefs,* IV (Berlin, 1968), pp. 204–07, no. 88. A thorough discussion of the sarcophagus can be found in Rubinstein 1976.
[59] Inv. 1874,0808.383, 29.5 × 42.7 cm; see Brussels/Kassel 2012–13, cat. 67, pp. 178–79.
[60] See Van der Meulen 1994. Rubens's interest in sarcophagi is attested not only by the early Christian exemplar that belonged to his own collection and his drawings after sarcophagi, but also the mention of a Roman Venus and Adonis sarcophagus from the late 2nd century AD (Rome, Palazzo Rospigliosi - Ex: collection of Tiberio Ceuoli, Villa Giulia) in the description of Rubens's Italian journey by his friend, the humanist Peiresc (Ms. Bib. Nat. Paris, MS Fr. 9530, fol. 200 recto. See Van der Meulen 1994, cat. nos. 132–42, and I, pp. 154–56.
[61] In Brussels/Kassel 2012–13, pp. 82–88, cat. 29, I examine Janssen's use of sarcophagus motifs in more detail.
[62] See the detailed explanation in Rubinstein 1976.
[63] See Muller 1982.
[64] Naples, Museo Archeologico Nazionale, Sala di Venere Callipigie, inv. 6020. In Jordaens's time it was still in the Palazzo Farnese in Rome.
[65] See Müller Hofstede 1971, pp. 208–303 and 300–01 (summary), esp. pp. 262–63.
[66] For ancient theories of imitation and Rubens's use of them, see Muller 1982.
[67] X-rays (January 10, 2012) and mosaic (February 2, 2012) by Catherine Fondaire (KIK).
[68] D'Hulst 1952, p. 28, and note 11, with reference to a similar supposition made by Held 1939, p. 19, as well as the suggestion that the Wallace Collection canvas was cut down from below.
[69] Letter with report dated 27 December 2010, no. 480, on our sample number AAR: 14551, by Dr. Jan Heinemeier, Director, AMS 14C Dating Centre, Institut for Fysik og Astronomi, Aarhus Universitet, held in the museum files.
[70] Report by Cecil Krarup Andersen, verified by Dr. Jørgen Wadum SMK (Statens Museum for Kunst) – CATS (Centre for Art Technological Studies and Conservation), held in the museum files (April 26, 2011).
[71] See the report by Steven Saverwyns, dossier no. 2009.10133, KIK-IRPA. The report was not conclusive due to impurities in the sample.
[72] Among the C-14 dates with the highest probability, that of ca. 1740 corresponds best to the history of the painting's provenance: relining would thus have occurred between the auction of the Della Faille collection in The Hague in 1730 and the sale of pictures from the painters' association Pictura in 1764. The 18th-century characteristics of the stretcher frame point in the same direction. It is possible, but statistically less likely, that the painting was relined around 1770, prior to the sale of the collection of Jan Spex, who worked for the administration of the Prince of Orange, in 1777.
[73] See my remarks in Brussels/Kassel 2012–13, pp. 165–69.
[74] This is one of the main theses of the exhibition Brussels/Kassel 2012–13.
[75] See Joaneath Spicer, "'De Koe voor d'aerde statt': The Origins of the Dutch Cattle Piece," in *Essays in Northern European Art Presented to Egbert Haverkamp-Begemann on his Sixthieth Birthday,* (Doornspijk, 1983), pp. 251–59 and 7 ill. See also n. 76.
[76] In book III, which is devoted to different kinds of flocks, as well as the breeding of horses and sheep.
[77] Díaz Padrón 1995, I, pp. 214–19. Padron's reference to another famous antique author, Hesiod, *Works and Days,* may turn out to be even more pertinent to Jordaens's interests than previously imagined, as Hesiod focuses on the right calendar for agricultural activities (see essay by Irene Schaudies in this volume).
[78] Inv. 1444; see Díaz Padrón 1995, I, pp. 214–19. See also Ertz 1979, pp. 494–99, and cat. 362, with references to Pieter I Bruegel as well as analogous drawings and painted motifs by Rubens. The painting entered the collection of

the queen of Spain, the first wife of Philip IV, in 1636. Previously, Archdukes Albert and Isabella had commissioned scenes of country life from Jan I Brueghel in which they mingled with rural folk in a sort of idealized variation on the realistic peasant scenes of Pieter Bruegel the Elder. Díaz Padrón rightly notes the dynastic importance of this sort of scene for princes: they were major landowners thanks to their ancient feudal claims. This kind of connection between agriculture and art deserves further investigation; up to now it has been limited to specific aspects such as Theeuwissen's study of agricultural tools, or the economic significance of cows in the Netherlands and Friesland. The theme of the earth's fertility in agriculture in (South) Netherlandish painting in the 17th century has yet to be studied as a general phenomenon.

[79] H. Barthélemy Aneau, AMORVM CONVERSIO AD STVDIA, in his emblem book *Picta Poesis*, Lyon, 1552 (A. Henkel & A. Schöne, *Emblemata: Handbuch zur Sinnbildkunst des XVI. und XVII.* Jahrhunderts, Stuttgart, 1967, column 1833).

[80] See my comments in Brussels/Kassel 2012, cat. 64, pp. 172–75.

[81] *Ibid.*

[82] See my essay in Brussels/Kassel 2012, pp. 165–69: *The Abundance of Peace.*

[83] They originally came from Kortrijk (Courtrai) in West-Flanders. See Y. Schmitz, Les Della Faille, I, *Des origines au XVII ième siècle*, Brussels, 1965.

[84] April 24, 1730. See my comments as in note 80, cat. 64.

[85] March 12, 1734. See Antwerp 1993, I, p. 21.

[86] A good indication of their collecting activities through the ages is their 1941 donation to the Royal Museums of Fine Arts of Belgium in Brussels. See: Marguerite Devigne, *Verzameling della Faille de Leverghem* (Brussels, 1944), especially the historical note on pp. 3–11, which also includes a list of other paintings which came from the same family but which were acquired by the museum separately on earlier occasions at public auctions.

[87] A telling example is their patronage of the chapel of the Brotherhood of the Holy Cross in the St Michael's Church in Ghent in the 1620s, when Jordaens was painting the Brussels allegory. See D. Roggen, "Het Caravaggisme te Gent," in *Gentse Bijdragen tot te Kunstgeschiedenis*, XII, Antwerp, 1949–50, p. 266; and Vander Auwera 2003, p. 501*ff.* In the same period they commissioned one of Abraham Janssen's most important altarpieces, the *Virgo inter virgins,* for the Antwerp church of the Shod Carmelites (now in the archbishoprical St John's Church in Lyon). See G. Chomer, "The 'Virgo inter Virgines' of Abraham Janssens," in *The Burlington Magazine* 221, no. 917 (August 1979), pp. 508–11, (ill opposite p. 471), and J. Vander Auwera, "Conservatieve tendenzen in de contrareformatorische kunst. Het geval Abraham Janssen," in *De zeventiende eeuw*, 1989, pp. 32–43, esp. p. 37.

[88] Norbert Schneider reaches a similar conclusion in "Wirtschafts- und sozialgeschichtliche Aspekte des Früchtenstillebens," in Münster 1979, p. 272, and Cologne 1990, pp. 28–29, although he mistakenly identifies one of the figures as Saturn with a supposed female patron: "Beaucoup de riches citadins avaient racheté des propriétés rurales aux nobles appauvris ... où ils faisaient travailler des tâcherons selon les nouvelles méthodes de production.... C'est ainsi que ce motif de corne d'abondance, répété dans ces tableaux de marchés, correspond davantage à la perception des personnes vivant de revenus agricoles, ainsi des fermiers nouveaux-riches.... Jacob Jordaens a réuni, dans son *Allégorie de la fécondité* ... divinités bachiques des champs et des bois ... ce tableau, qui est destine à honorer la croissance de la production sur sa propriéré seigneurale avec des formules du pathos de la mythologie antique."

II. Technical Analysis

Observations Made During the Conservation Treatment of Jordaens's *Allegory of Fruitfulness* from the Wallace Collection

VICTORIA SUTCLIFFE, ANNA SANDÉN

The conservation and restoration of the Wallace Collection's *Allegory of Fruitfulness* used several analytical techniques including X-ray, cross section analysis, and of course, visual examination. All of these tools threw new light onto the working methods of Jordaens. The most captivating observation is that the Wallace Collection canvas was used more than once, and that the execution of a complete version of the newly conserved *Allegory of Fertility* in Brussels (pp. 6–7), lies beneath the *Allegory of Fruitfulness* (pp. 12–13).

The conservation history of the *Allegory of Fruitfulness* is unknown but the painting was probably cleaned in the nineteenth century and is likely to have been relined with glue paste and placed onto a new stretcher prior to its purchase by Sir Richard Wallace in 1872. This would date the relining canvas to ca. 1850–70. It measures 201 × 229.5 cm, and the original canvas is made from two pieces of canvas with a central seam where, almost certainly, the two selvedges have been bound together. (In comparison, the Brussels painting is also made from two pieces of canvas with a central seam, but measures 180 × 341 cm, somewhat more horizontal in format.) There is slight cusping visible on all aor less retained its original size.

A horizontal line of repeated damage across the upper half of the painting may indicate that it was once rolled and compressed, while the damages around the periphery suggest that the edge of the painting was once used as the tacking margin. The canvas has also sustained a large vertical tear through the crouching satyr's chest which could have been the initial reason for lining the painting. These losses of original paint and associated fills can be observed on the X-ray. Fortunately, the losses do not disrupt any key paint passages and little reconstruction was required to re-incorporate the image during conservation.

The Artist's Palette and the Structure of the Paint Layers

Although the analysis of the artist's palette shows the use of a standard range of materials and techniques for the first half of the seventeenth century, it could be seen from the richly

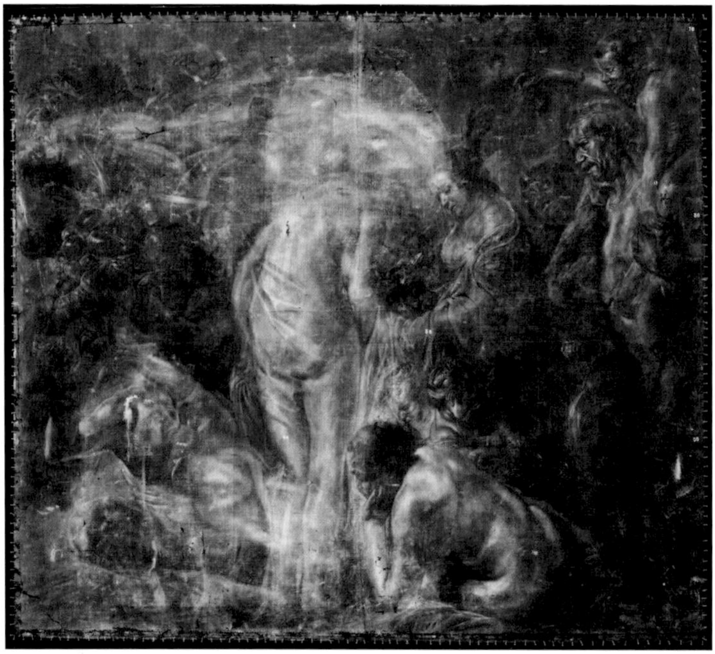

35. X-ray image of *Allegory of Fruitfulness* (Reproduced by kind permission of the Trustees of the Wallace Collection; X-ray taken by Rachel Billinge, National Gallery, London)

colored paint passages, even before the varnish was removed, that Jordaens's palette consisted of high quality, pigment-rich paints. The bold colors contrast with each other across the painting, from the rich blue of the sky to the bright red of the drapery and the freshness of the whites.

Several cross-sections were taken to gain a better understanding of the layer structure and pigments used.[1] A grey ground, consisting of charcoal black and lead white pigment particles, has been applied directly onto a light lower ground made mainly of chalk. This grey ground appears to consist of graduated shades, as in some areas it appears dark, such as under the sky, and in other areas light, such as under the central area of the cornucopia. This ground can most easily be seen around the grapes and other fruit where thin paint layers are painted directly over a light grey and have not been modified between the first and second compositions. In other areas the grey ground is less visible, due to the multiple layers applied on top, but plays a key role in lending translucency to some of the flesh tones, which remain largely unaltered between the two compositions; for instance, throughout the crouching woman's back. Underdrawing could not be detected during infra-red examination, which may be due to the obscuring nature of the generally thick paint layers. However, some possible traces of underdrawing, consisting of thin black lines, are visible under one area of the cornucopia (figs. 36, 37).

Several different blues have been used by Jordaens. The blue of the sky, for example, is a high quality azurite, but this has been made even brighter in the second campaign of painting by applying a second layer of high quality azurite containing less lead white. The second application of sky blue can be most clearly seen applied around the heads of the central

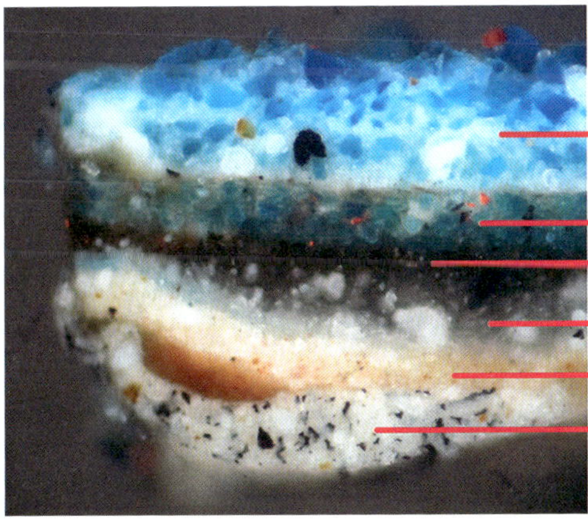

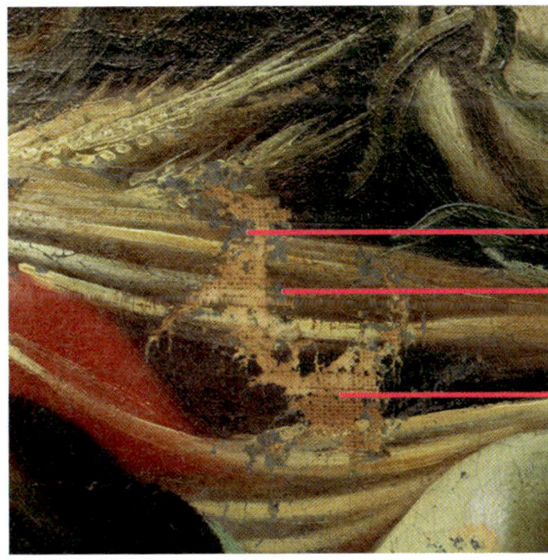

36. Detail of *An Allegory of Fruitfulness*
Cross section taken from the sky, lower left corner. A. Grey upper ground. B. Pale pink/brown. C. Indigo and lead white. D. Translucent mixed brown. E. Azurite. F. Azurite and lead white. (Image courtesy of Libby Sheldon, London)

37. Cross section 2
Detail of corn stalks and heads in the cornucopia. A. Some thin lines of dark underdrawing. B. Light grey of ground. C. Area of loss. (Anna Sandén, reproduced by kind permission of the Trustees of the Wallace Collection)

standing figures. Blue verditer has been used, mixed with yellow lake to create the green tones of the foliage. The most puzzling use of blue, however, has been applied below the flesh of the crouching satyr in the lower left corner of the painting. This is a very dark indigo and became visible after overpaint and fill were removed from losses to the upper flesh tones of the satyr (fig. 39).

The red of the drapery remains relatively unchanged between the two compositions and consists of a bright layer of vermilion applied directly to the grey ground, with a thick layer of organic red glaze. It is in the reds that the quality of the pigments attests to the continued condition of the tones of the paint layers. The red lake has faded in the uppermost layers, but due to its thickness and high quality vermilion underneath, it remains visibly bright and rich. Vermilion has also been used, mixed with a lead-based yellow, to create the orange hues of the fruit. The alteration of the white fabric to the bottom of the painting, however, has not withstood the test of time so well. A blue and red layer has been added here, presumably as part of the second composition, to create a purple that has now discolored to brown (fig. 41).

The painting has, of course, aged in various ways through abrasions from old restoration campaigns, physical damage, and increased transparency as well as through the fading of more fugitive pigments. This can be most clearly seen in the central nude figure's knee, where increased transparency of the leg of the second composition has made the pentiment of the back of the leg below more obvious. In the lower area of the painting in particular, the abrasion from previous over-cleaning strongly contributes to the appearance of the painting, more so than natural ageing factors. Several areas are worn, such as the areas around the

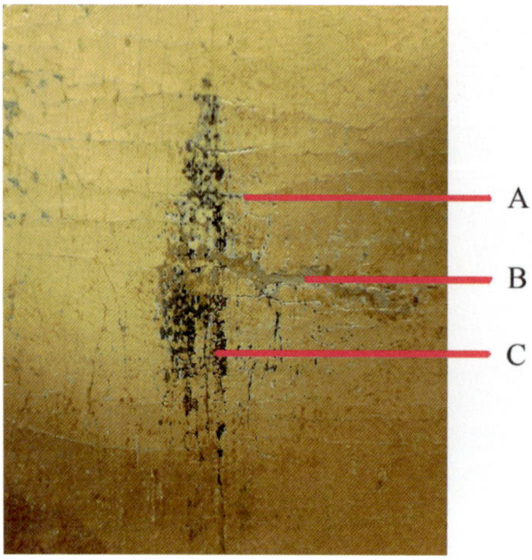

39. Detail of a loss in the crouching satyrs chest (after varnish removal). A. Grey ground layer. B. Grey fill material within loss. C. Dark indigo layer beneath flesh tones.
(Anna Sandén, reproduced by kind permission of the Trustees of the Wallace Collection)

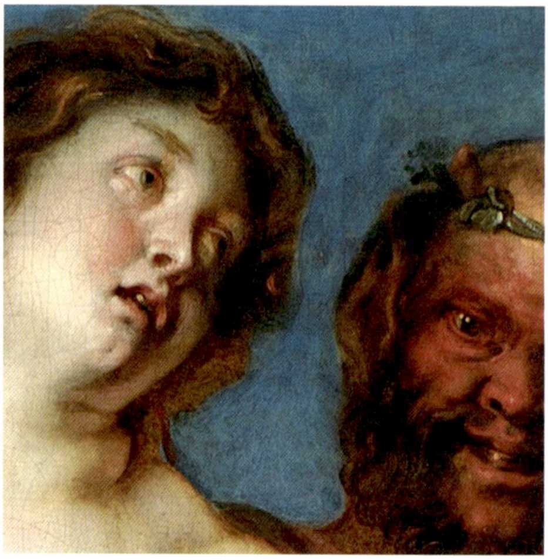

40. Detail of *An Allegory of Fruitfulness* after conservation showing the rapid and broad brush strokes of the blue sky of the seond composition.
(Anna Sandén, reproduced by kind permission of the Trustees of the Wallace Collection)

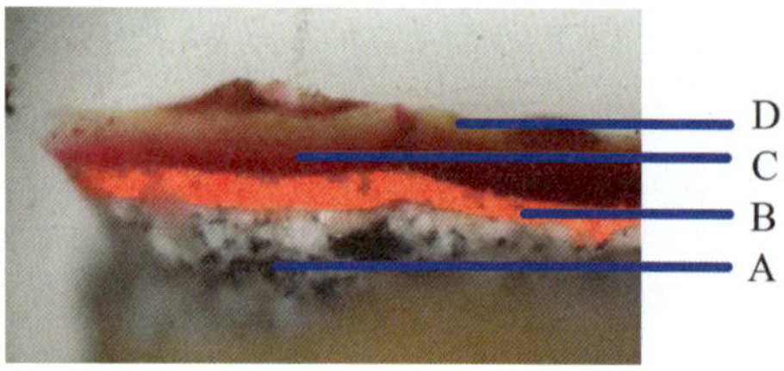

41. Detail 4 of *An Allegory of Fruitfulness* after conservation.
Cross section taken from the red drapery showing: A. the grey upper ground; B. A vermilion layer and a layer of red glaze (C) which has faded towards the top (D). (Image courtesy of Libby Sheldon, London)

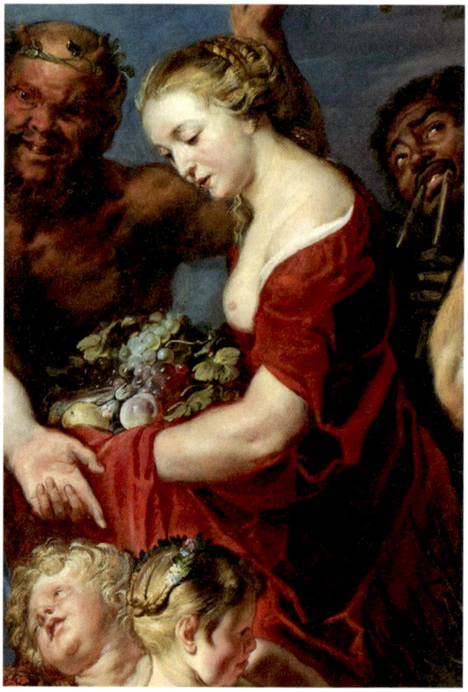

42. Detail of the *Allegory of Fruitfulness* showing the richness of the red drapery. (Anna Sandén, reproduced by kind permission of the Trustees of the Wallace Collection)

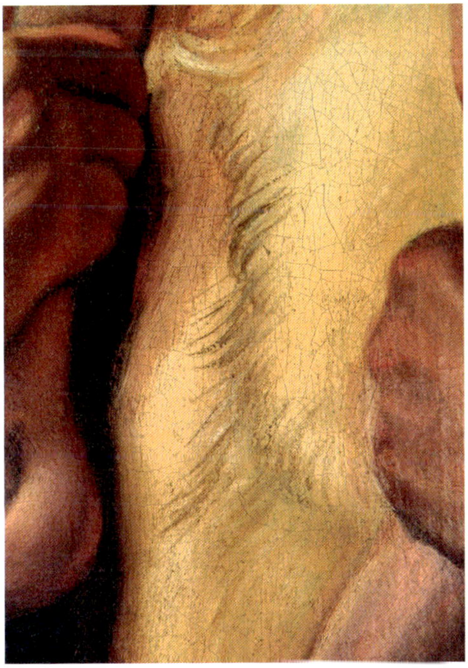

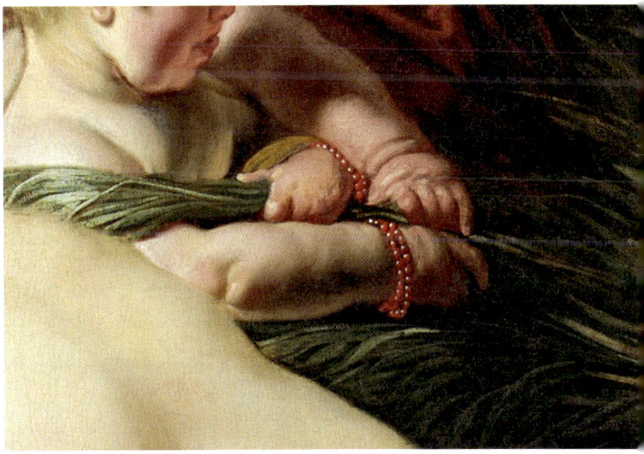

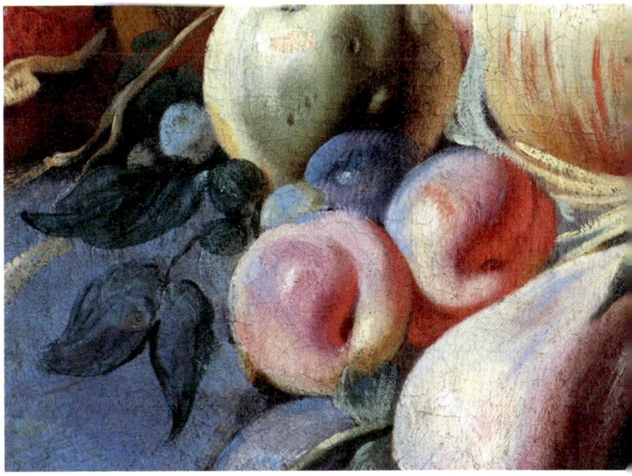

43. Details of *An Allegory of Fruitfulness* after conservation; detail of the thickly painted reeds; the chest of the standing satyr showing reticulation of the paint used to depict hairs; detail of the cornucopia, showing the paint handling and changes in composition. (Anna Sandén, reproduced by kind permission of the Trustees of the Wallace Collection)

legs of both the central standing figure and the crouching satyr. The two layered composition may have been the reason for this over-cleaning. The past restoration campaigns are numerous, as indicated by the number of different fill materials and overpaint discovered during cleaning. Past restoration campaigns applied several layers of varnish which had become darkened and discolored.

The application of the visible layers of paint is dictated not only by the color of the lower paint layers, but also by their texture. A wide range of different paint characteristics can be found on the painting. In the areas of revision between the first and second compositions the paint handling is much more rapid, confident, and loose, as can be seen, for example, in the rendering of Silenus in comparison to the flesh of the standing satyr to the right, or the application of the sweeping sky in comparison to the more delicately modeled fruit.

In most areas wet-in-wet paint layers have been used to define depth and shape with a variety of brush strokes. In the fruit in particular, modelling has sometimes been carried out with

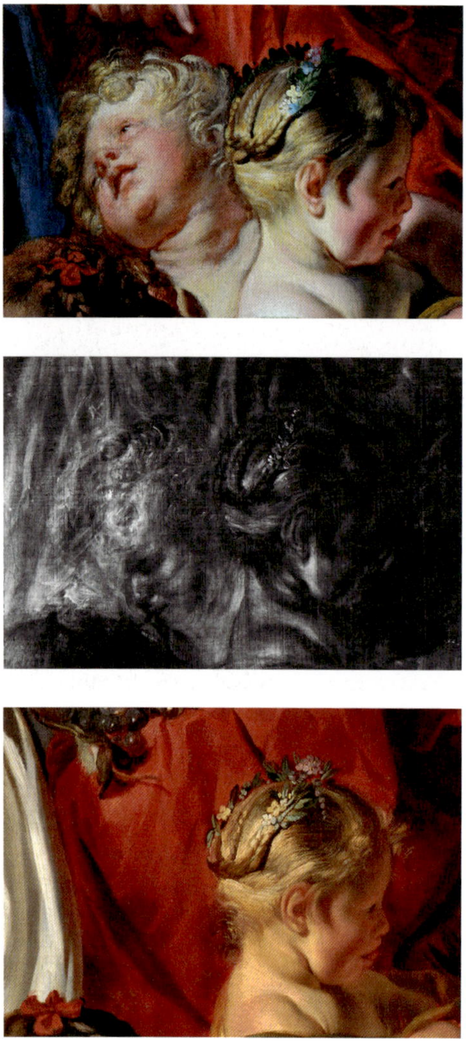

45. Details of *An Allegory of Fruitfulness* (after conservation) with its X-ray and *An Allegory of Fertility*, showing the changing position of the left child. (Anna Sandén, reproduced by kind permission of the Trustees of the Wallace Collection) (X-ray reproduced by kind permission of the Trustees of the Wallace Collection; X-ray taken by Rachel Billinge, National Gallery, London)

the use of small lines to mix opposing colors to gain a sense of shape. Some areas of yellow, green, and red glaze can be seen in the vegetation and on the red drapery. Drier, thicker paint has been used to create the sweeping reeds moved aside by the children. Here, the brush strokes have caught on the lower paint layers and have created a textured appearance where glazes have collected in their hollows.

The paint layers are generally thick and pigment rich as seen in the cross sections but thin and more dilute paint applications can be seen in several areas such as in the thin yellow glaze on the skin of the crouching woman or in the long lines of dark paint that can be seen dripping down the dark vegetation in the lower right corner. This indicates that the oil glaze layers were probably diluted before application. Reticulation of a dark brown layer, used mainly to depict hairs, can clearly be seen on the standing satyr's chest. This characteristic may have occurred if the lower layer was dry when a thin and quite liquid oil paint was applied on top (fig. 43).

Compositional Changes

The results of the paint samples, X-ray, and observation of the paint surface itself suggest that the execution of a version of *An Allegory of Fertility* is complete beneath the now visible *Allegory of Fruitfulness*. Examination also suggests there is no intermediate layer between the two; on the contrary, the lower layer has been used to play a key role in the aesthetics of the upper paint layers. This can most clearly be observed in the standing woman's face. Clearly some abrasion and increased transparency have occurred in this area, but the first composition is seen to such an extent that it is likely to have been used by the artist as a tool to depict the shadow of the face.

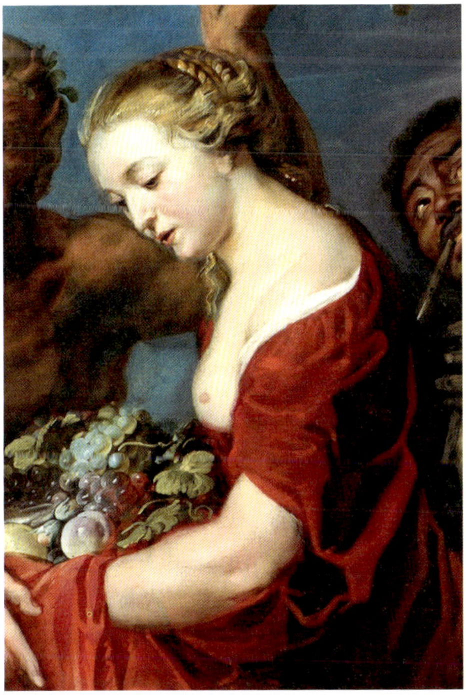

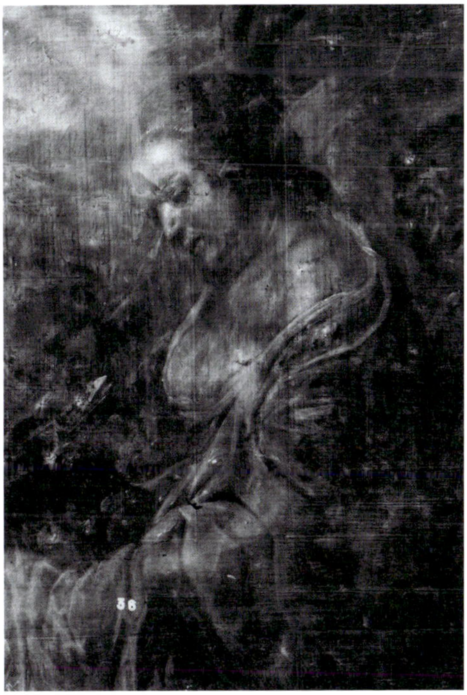

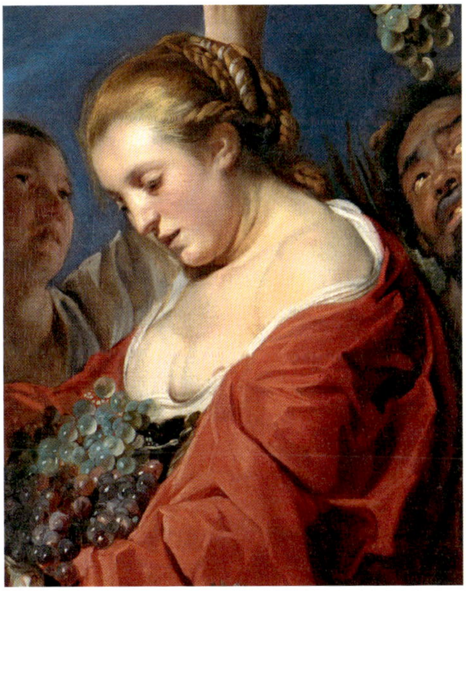

46. Details of *An Allegory of Fruitfulness* with its X-ray and *An Allegory of Fertility*, showing the changing proportions of the woman in red. (Anna Sandén, reproduced by kind permission of the Trustees of the Wallace Collection) (X-ray reproduced by kind permission of the Trustees of the Wallace Collection; X-ray taken by Rachel Billinge, National Gallery, London) (Royal Museums of Fine Arts of Belgium).

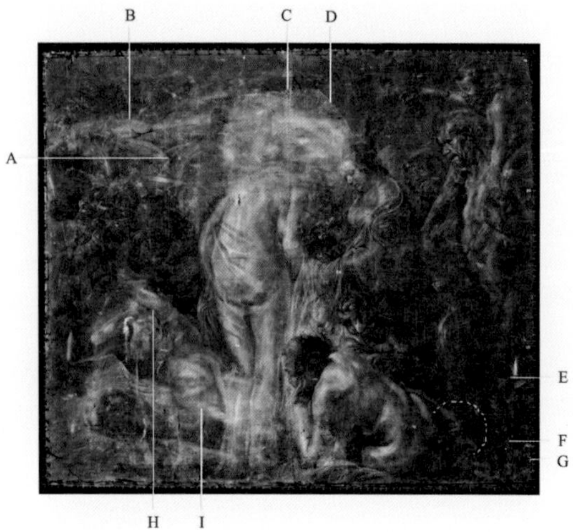

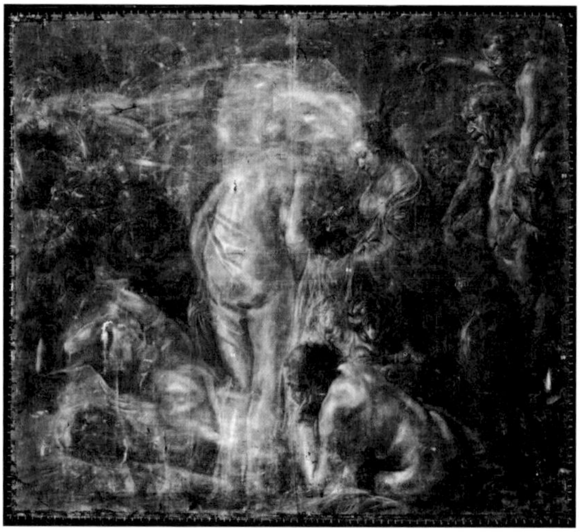

47. Illustrated X-ray image of the *Allegory of Fruitfulness.* A. palette knife scrapings. B. Viewed at 90 degrees anti-clockwise, the legs of the central standing nude. C. The upper body of the central standing nude. D. Palette knife scrapings associated with the standing nude? E, F and G Palette knife scrapings. H. Viewed at 180 degrees, a sleeved hand. I. Indecipherable shape beneath satyr's chest. (Reproduced by kind permission of the Trustees of the Wallace Collection; X-ray taken by Rachel Billinge, National Gallery, London)

The many pentimenti are due to the interaction between the upper and lower compositions, but some are possibly changes made in the upper composition alone. As Lucy Davis has pointed out, the main areas of change include the reorientation of the central nude figure; the inclusion of the small boy; the substitution of the woman behind the central nude figure for Silenus; and the change of the standing woman from old to young. Many smaller, more detailed changes have also been made between the first and second compositions. However, some changes may have been made solely within the upper layer, such as the repositioning of the small boy from facing downward to facing upward, as this figure is completely absent from the Brussels painting. The arm of the woman in red has been painted over the red drapery, so that it is now more in proportion to the Brussels version torso, which may indicate her arm was added and her torso altered in two separate stages (fig. 46).

By comparing the painting with the X-ray, many aspects of change within the picture can be observed. The X-ray clearly shows several re-workings on the canvas that do not relate either to the first or second compositions. In the lower right corner possible palette knife marks can be seen as if a new ground has been applied over an earlier image. In the lower left corner, under the crouching satyr, the X-ray layer structure is difficult to interpret as if, again, changes have been made. Viewed in a 90-degree rotation, the possible figure of the standing woman can be seen to the left of the painting, with more possible palette markings around her. Viewed at 180 degrees, brush strokes resembling a sleeved arm and hand can also be seen beneath the crouching satyr. The X-ray image of the head of the woman in red bears an uncanny resemblance to the woman who has been painted out of *The Tribute Money* (canvas II) but is still visible in the X-ray

(Statens Museum for Kunst, Copenhagen),[2] reinforcing the notion that Jordaens reused images throughout his lifetime. Other details are visible on the painting that correspond neither with the two compositions nor the X-ray, for example, the distinct circular shape in the lower right corner (fig. 47).

It was a rare opportunity to be able to view the two closely related paintings by Jordaens, the *Allegory of Fruitfulness* from the Wallace Collection in London and the *Allegory of Fertility* from the Royal Museums of Fine Arts of Belgium in Brussels. In light of the intriguing exhibition *Jordaens and the Antique,* which has renewed interest in Jordaens's oeuvre, we hope the discoveries highlighted in this article can add to the discussion on the artist's painting technique and working methods.

[1] Pigment analysis carried out by Libby Sheldon, London.
[2] Copenhagen 2008, pp. 71–72.

Restoration Report on Jacques Jordaens's *Allegory of Fertility*, Royal Museums of Fine Arts of Belgium

PHAM THANH-NGHI

General State of Conservation

Support

The support is composed of two pieces of which the vertical seam is situated in the middle of the composition, and visible on the painted surface (fig. 48).

Slight deformations situated on the lower left corner. During treatment of the work, which was unframed in the museum's restoration studio, these deformations diminished. Could this improvement have been due to the fact that the support was in a location where the humidity level was more constant, and higher than in the location where it is usually exhibited?

The borders have been cut: the format of the work has been subject to modification (shortening).

Along the entire length of the lower border, one finds an added strip of around 3 cm. In consultation with the curators of the Museum, it was decided to retain this addition (fig. 49).

2

Presence of lining applied with paste. The lining canvas is composed of two pieces, of which the horizontal seam marks the paint layer and is located at 70–72 cm from the lower edge.

The joint (seam) of these two pieces is visible on the unpainted canvas folded over the sides of the stretcher frame.

The edges of the lining canvas have been cut at the edge of the stretcher frame. Because of this, it would be necessary to add a strip-lining (additions to the canvas under tension) if one wants to retain the canvas (fig. 50).

3 Stretcher Frame

The stretcher frame with keys is made of pine and furnished with two uprights. The construction is mortise and tenon. Unfortunately it is somewhat weak in relation to the size of the painting, particularly given the relining. The absence of cross-pieces appears to be detrimental, because the frame is slightly warped. In accordance with the section of the frame, it needs two cross-pieces to ensure maximum structural stability.

The keys of the uprights have been driven in excessively (to better tighten the canvas), to the point that the upper extremities of the uprights are cracked.

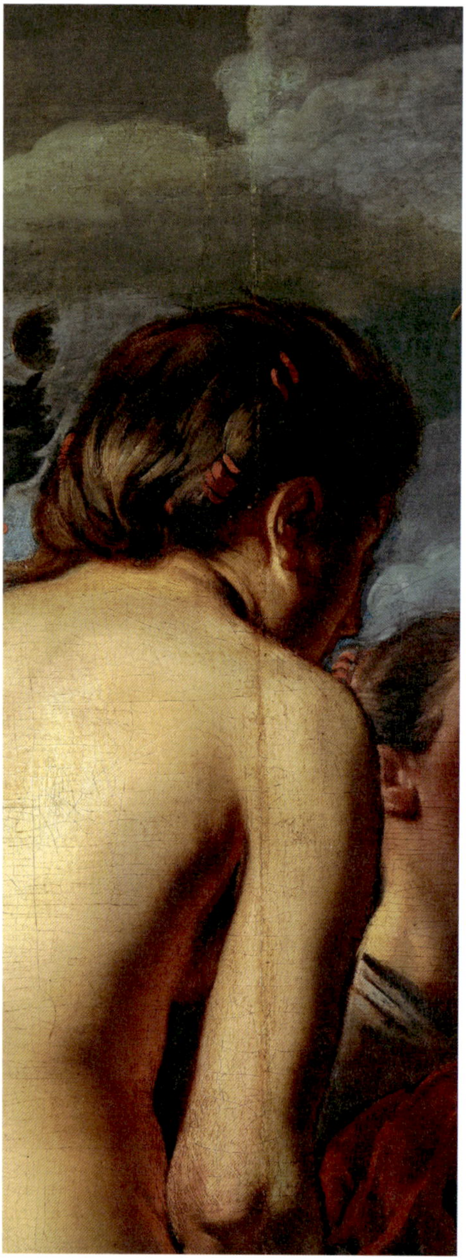

48. Detail of the nymph
seen from behind
in the foreground,
with vertical seam

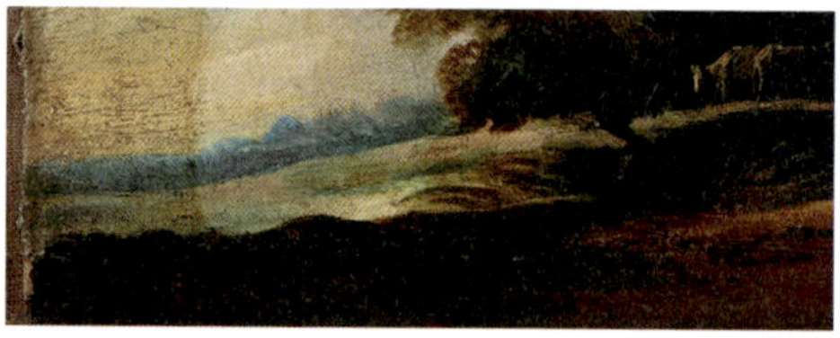

49. Lower border

4

As is the lower extremity of the right lateral bar, when facing the frame. The cracks have been re-glued with acetate polyvinyl (PVA).

5

After lining, the work was attached to the stretcher using nails. On the sides of the stretcher frame, there are no other visible marks indicating that the lining canvas was otherwise attached.

This means that after relining, the oeuvre has remained attached to the same stretcher frame ever since; it has never been removed. Hence, the relining was carried out towards the middle of the 18th century (information provided by the Museum, letter of 26.08.2011; ref.: MD/JVA/ADM), and the chassis must therefore have been made in the same period. If this is the case, we have on our hands a rare example of a keyed stretcher frame dating to the 18th century. And this crucial observation necessarily leads us to consider – or reconsider – certain aspects of the treatment (see Proposed Treatment).

The placement of the nails fixing the canvas was carried out cleanly and remains perfectly intact: it would be *impossible* to remove the nails and put them back in the same place *without damaging the heads*, the canvas, and the stretcher frame itself. The absence of other traces of fixation *on the lining canvas* is the most tangible confirmation that the chassis and the lining date to the same period. It may be argued that there are traces of earlier fixations underneath the lining canvas, but no evidence to this effect has been discovered. Moreover, if such traces did in fact exist, it would bluntly refute this casual suggestion, because it would mean that the frame had already been used *before* the stretching of the present canvas – in other words, that the stretcher was *even older* than the lining (that is, that it was made *before* the canvas was relined).

6 Paint Layer

Lifting in several places, which is made visible by the elevated ridges of the craquelure. It is found in the following areas:

Sky in the lower left corner of the composition
Vine leaves in the lower left corner
wo arms and knee of the kneeling satyr at the left
Legs of the central female figure (standing)
Along the length of the vertical seam
Right hand and left arm of the woman seated in the foreground
And numerous other places (fig. 51).

Shortly after beginning the process of fixation, we noticed that the lifting was more copious than anticipated in the pre-treatment report: at the intersection of the craquelure, the fine ridges were standing straight.

Unless fixed, these ridges would be caught by the fibers of the swab and torn by the motions of cleaning. For this reason, it was necessary to re-fix 85% of the painted surface.

7

In relation to the sizable dimensions of the work, the areas of retouching are comparatively few, and are found primarily along the four edges.

The upper left corner of the sky was almost completely covered with overpainting, which could be distinguished by the fact that it had darkened, and by the screen-like effect resulting from the way it covered the network of craquelure.

Along the upper edge, the overpainting reached as far as 3 to 6 cm in places, and were always applied in those areas of the sky or clouds that form contours around other elements, such as leaves and fruit ... and finishing in the upper right corner with parallel bands along the edges.

8

In fact, the overpainting turned out to be more important than anticipated. In effect, nearly the entire sky above the figures had been completely painted over. This overpainting, grayish-blue in tone, covered the original with a thick layer, opaque where it followed approximately the shapes of the original clouds (fig. 52). In removing it, we found the remains of earlier overpainting, but also some abrasions in the paint layer where the colors corresponded to and harmonized with the intense blue of the original sky.

The colors used to paint the sky are the same used by the artist in several of his compositions, notably the *Pan and Syrinx* (inv. 3292) in the collection of the Museum: in a diagonal running from the lower left corner, the sky is a light blue, which, traveling upwards, becomes more and more intensely colored until it becomes blue-black in the upper right corner.

9

While the painting's state of conservation is considered excellent, it is not clear why the presence of overpainting in the flesh-tones is concentrated exclusively in the legs of the female figure seen from behind. In effect, from her hip down to the base of her calves, we find heavy-handed

50. Right border of the stretcher with (left to right) the edge of the original canvas and of the lining canvas

interventions in the shadows, particularly those of the right leg, and the remains of earlier overpainting in very small patches. Examination under UV light confirms that some kind of sauce was applied to these zones in order to mask the irregularity of the overpainting. Fortunately, this material was easy to remove, because it was situated at the level of the varnish. But the overpainting was very difficult to eliminate, to dislodge from the hollows of the brushstrokes (fig. 59).

10

Overpainting is also visible on certain leaves of the cherry, red-currant and vines, as well as some of the stalks of the plants behind the woman in red (figs. 53, 55).

There are few lacunae, but the largest is found over the clavicle of the satyr crouching at the left (fig. 61). It is retouched in tempera, and extends beyond the original; however, it is also placed over a dark ground with craquelure that is well integrated into that of the paint layer. It is precisely this dark brown material that was used to fill in the lacuna instead of a traditional mastic made of chalk and animal glue, and that has resulted in a nice craquelure in the retouching that is almost identical to the craquelure in the original paint layer. It is, thus, a technique for creating artificial craquelure. In itself, this procedure is not difficult, but obtaining successful results is another story … a story of professional secrets. It should also be pointed out that this is not an isolated case, for we have already encountered other works in the Museum's collection during restoration that have been similarly retouched, among them *The Nativity with Donor and the Circumcision*, from the circle of Colijn de Coter (inv. 364, 2005-06), and the *Pietà* of Rogier van der Weyden (inv. 3515, 2008-09). In each case, the dark brown material is situated under the retouching. In the case of our Jordaens, it has been preserved along with one of the earlier instances of retouching

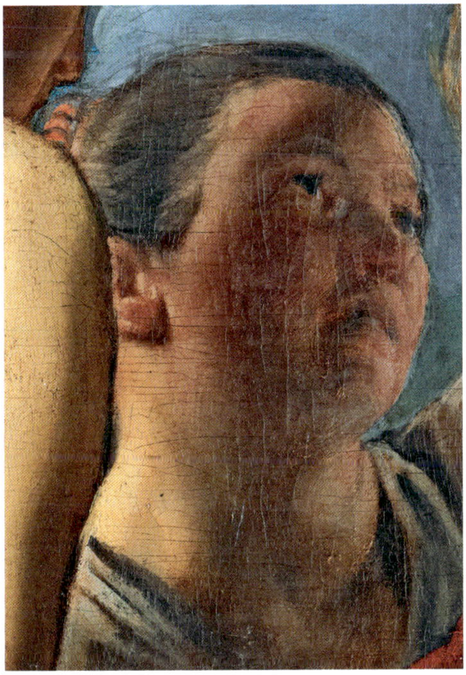

51. Head of the standing nymph in the background: lifting of the paint layer

(which has been altered by fresh retouching), in part to bear witness to the constantly changing process of restoration, and in part to record an instance of technical prowess without fear of harming the work's authenticity.

In a general way, the paint layer still remains in a very good state of conservation. Infrequent abrasions have been noted, such as the ridges of the underlying brushstrokes situated on the hair of the dark-skinned satyr in the middle ground.

11

After removing the overpainting from the sky (above the figures) and the legs of the large female figure seen from behind (fig. 59), other abrasions were revealed, which were more numerous in the zones just mentioned. Together with the remains of earlier overpainting (which were left in place because they were too difficult to remove), they are the reason for the presence of overpainting.

Abrasions can also be observed in the area around the signature, which is for this reason very discreet. It is situated at the very bottom of the cornucopia held in the left hand of the crouching satyr. Examination under UV gives it a more distinct aspect (figs. 33–36).

Other abrasions are to be found on the ridges of the brushstrokes in the blue sky situated at the level of the ears of grain between the elbow and knee of the crouching satyr.

12

The original (vertical) seam (fig. 48) was undoubtedly pressed toward the front by the relining and has become more visible, not only with the passage of time, but also thanks to the darkening of earlier retouches. The new mastication and the new retouching has greatly improved its appearance.

As said, the lower portion of the composition has also been cut, where an added strip of approximately 3 cm is visible to the naked eye. Its overpainting extends beyond the original by about 2 cm in places (fig. 49). In consultation with the curators of the Museum, the decision was made to preserve this addition with its overpainting, while adjusting the areas that had become too visually distracting as a result of darkening.

13

The presence of sauces used to "warm" the coloring by giving it an "old" appearance. The sauces that were most difficult to remove were found on the leaves of the artichoke, where the excess has dripped in places.

Some changes to the composition are partly

52. Upper left corner with overpainting forming contours around the clouds

53. Upper left corner with overpainting forming contours around leaves and fruit

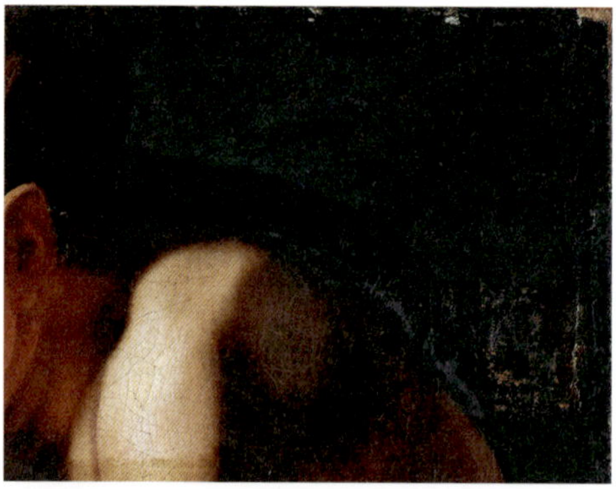

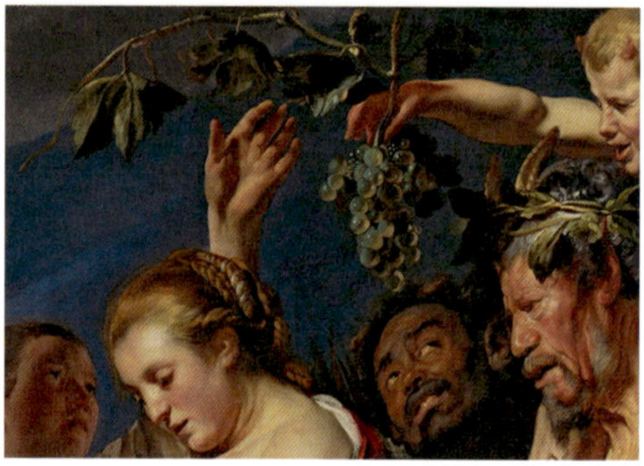

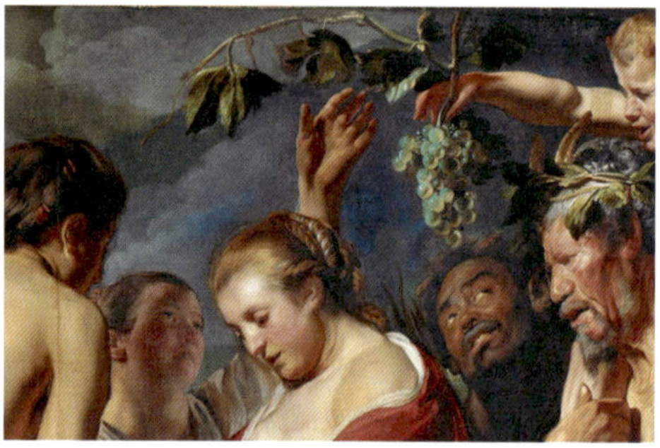

54. Upper right corner with overpainting forming contours around the boys body

55. Upper right part before cleaning

56. Idem, during treatment

visible to the naked eye, but they are very discreet and merge with the abundance of brushstrokes in bright colors; hence they do not disturb the overall appearance of the work.

If the changes to the composition, the retouching and underlying drawing are visible to the naked eye, there is another chemical phenomenon that may be detected as well; namely, saponification. This chemical reaction takes place between the fatty acids of the oil and the lead compounds (lead white, lead tin yellow, and red lead (minium) to form metal soaps (organic alkaline compounds). A highly interesting study by Silvia A. Centeno and Dorothy Mahon ("The Chemistry of Aging in Oil Paintings: Metal Soaps and Visual Changes," *Metropolitan Museum Journal* 40, 2005, pp. 12–19) provides us with ample explanation.

57. Detail of fig. 55
before treatment

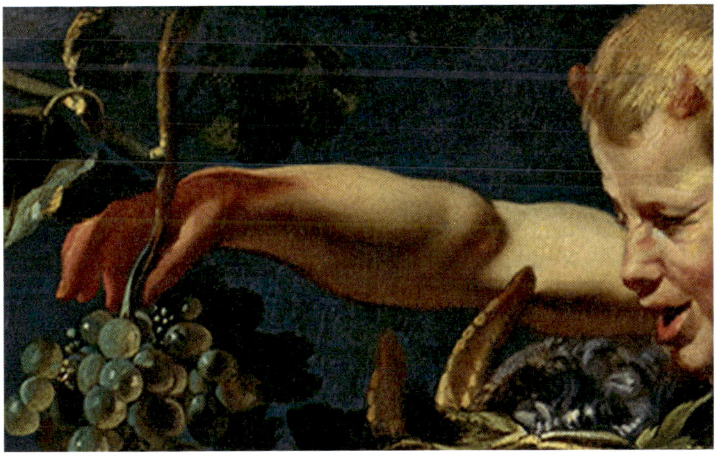

58. Right half of the sky
is revealed

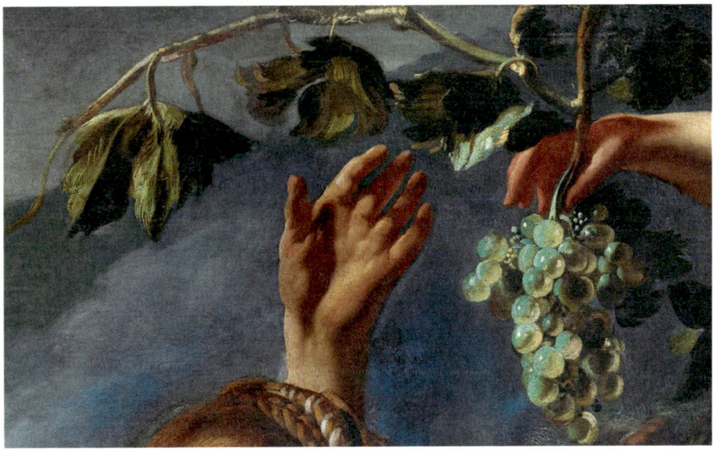

Saponification is detectable on sight by small, rounded points which literally penetrate the paint layer, as it were. In the Jordaens they manifest in various locations. The use of binocular magnifying glasses greatly aids observation. Because these elements form an integral part of the painting, they should not be removed (by scraping, for example). If they become problematic, light retouching is all that is needed to camouflage their presence. It might also be pointed out that saponification can be found in many works in the Museum's collection.

– Varnish
– Pronounced yellowing
– Presence of matte areas
– Scratches resulting from application of sauces, dust, incrusted yellow varnishes in countless crevices between brushstrokes (figs. 42–45), not only emphasize the overall darkening of the picture, but also necessitate intense cleaning.

15 Treatment

– Fixation of lifting: to provide new and better adherence of the paint layer to its support.

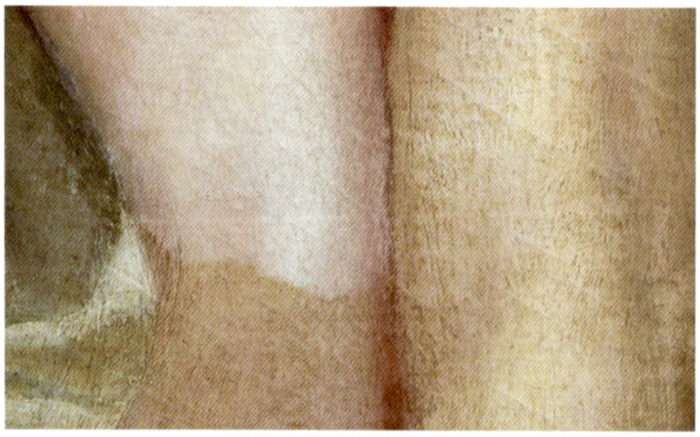

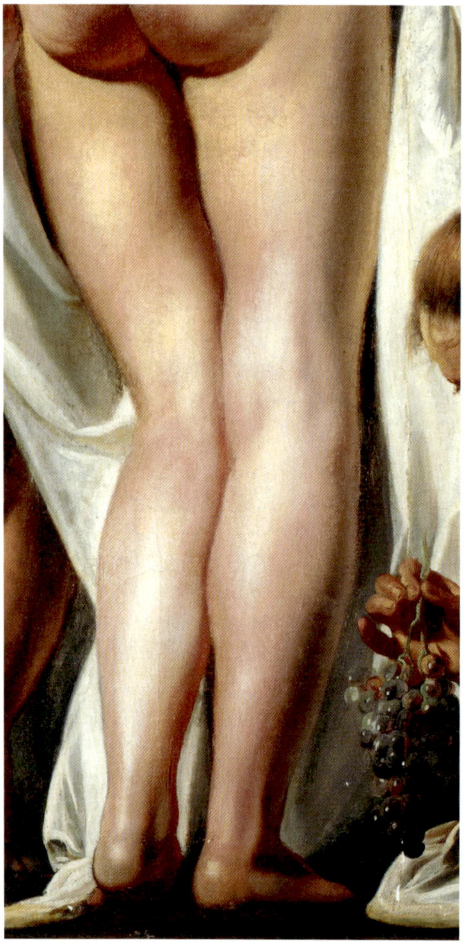

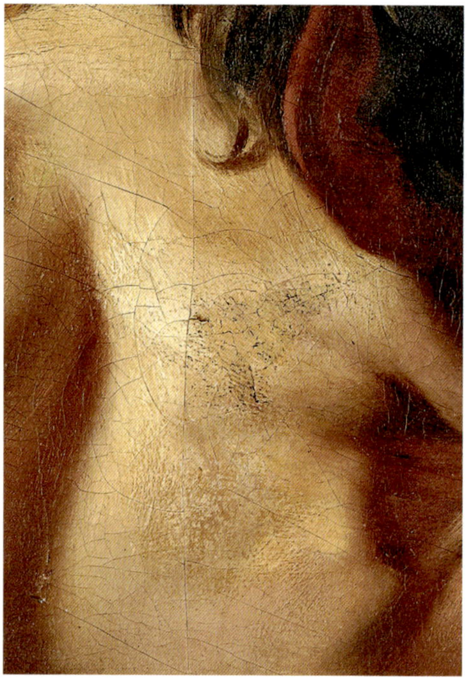

61. Detail of the satyr crouching at the left, during treatment

59. Legs of the nude nymph seen from behind in the foreground, during treatment

60. Idem, a more complete view, after treatment

The operation permits among other things the safe manipulation of the work, and was carried out in two phases: before and after cleaning. Experience often shows that worn varnish serving as a covering impedes the passage of the adhesive and makes fixation less effective, or not effective at all. If necessary a second fixation was carried out after removal of the varnish to ensure a better result. The fixation was carried out using a wax-resin.

– No intervention with respect to the slight deformation of the lower right corner of the support, for the following reasons:

– In relation to the overall tension and the large dimensions of the support, these deformations do not endanger either the pictorial surface or the aesthetic aspect of the work.

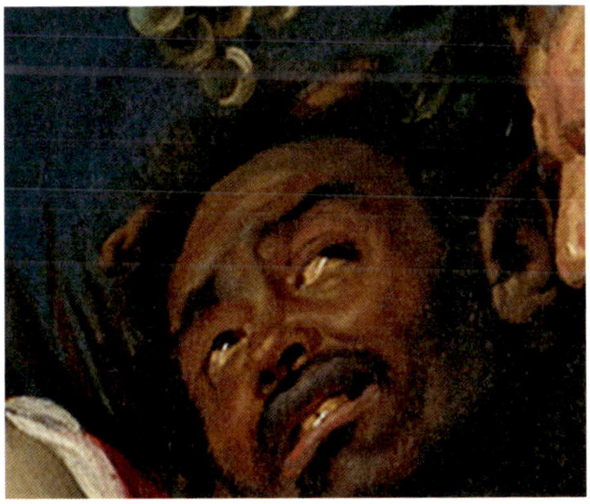

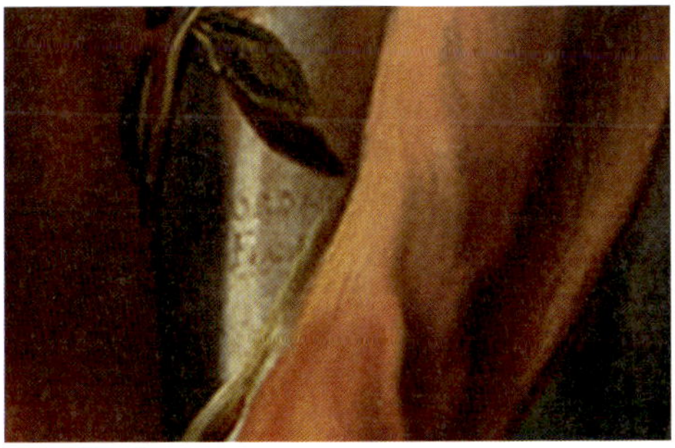

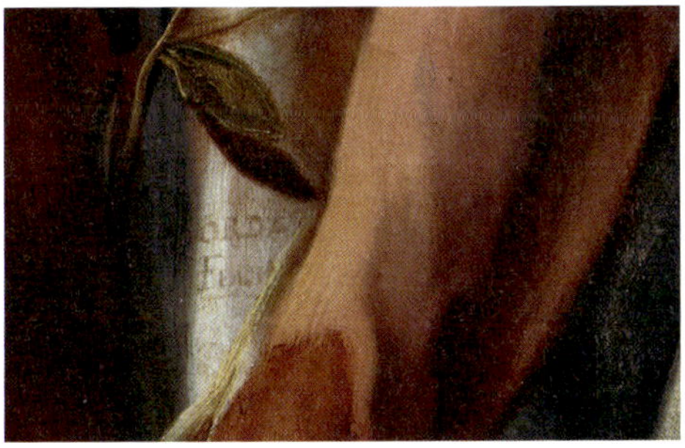

62. Detail of the dark-skinned satyr in the middle ground

63. Detail of the bottom of the cornucopia, before cleaning

64. Idem, after cleaning

– In forgoing improvement of the canvas tension, when all is said and done, relatively speaking, one privileges non-modification and thereby preserves every aspect, every authentic proof of an 18th-century relining and stretcher. This is probably a unique example in the Museum's collection, and will certainly stand out as such.

– Non-intervention in the case of the deformations of the canvas will neither impede nor prevent procedures from being carried out in the future if the need arises.

– Removal of the varnish. The varnish was resinous and remains soluble. It removal was effected with:

Ethanol – Iso-propanol 1:2
Iso-propanol – Iso-octane 1:1
Iso-propanol – Iso-octane 1:2

– Removal of overpainting, executed in tempera:
Dichloremethane – Ethyl acetate – Formic acid 50:50:1
Iso-propanol – Iso-octane 1:1
Iso-propanol – Iso-octane 1:2

– Mastication of lacunae carried out with chalk and animal glue

– Retouching of lacunae and abrasions in two phases to ensure reversibility: in watercolor to begin with, followed by Paraloid B72 mixed with pigments. Between the two phases, application of an intermediary, Dammar-based varnish.

For the flesh tints, it is important to underscore that the retouching was carried out exclusively in watercolor. This technique has great advantages:

– the watercolor does not yellow over time because it contains no resin
– it allows for a play of light and transparence
– by accommodating itself perfectly to the existing paint layer, it does not create excess thickness. It is precisely the use of extremely fine layers and play of transparency that makes this manner of retouching suited to areas of delicate flesh tones.
– it is completely reversible

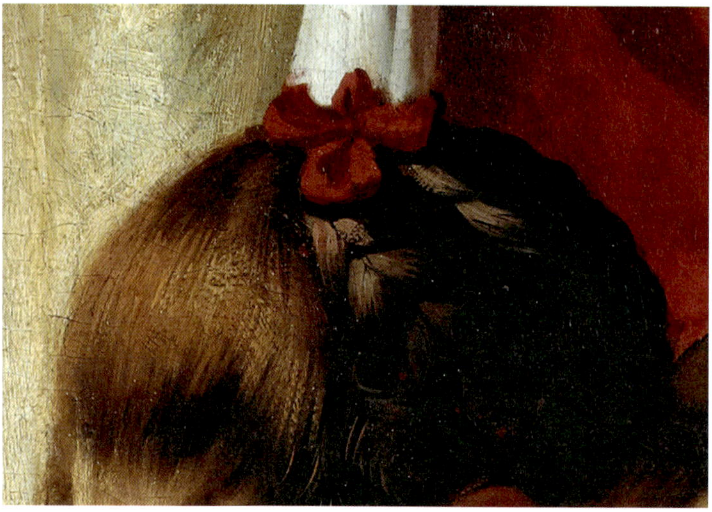

65. Detail with vegetables in the cornucopia at the upper left, with artichoke

66. Detail with the hair of the seated woman to the right, with rounded dark points due to saponification

– its complete reversibility makes the use of solvents unnecessary, without danger to the painted surface.

On the other hand, the employment of this technique proves to be difficult and time consuming in terms of execution.

16

– Application of a new Dammar-based varnish in two phases: initially with a brush, after retouching with watercolor; subsequently with a spray gun after retouching in Paraloid B72.

– Placement of a backboard

– Fixation of lifting and gluing detached parts of the frame with PVA (polyvinyl acetate)

– Dusting of the frame

– Gluing of the cracks in the stretcher bars with PVA

– Production of report on the treatment with 79 photos.

Conclusion

Each restoration is a privileged moment for studying a work in depth and extending our knowledge of it. The treatment of Jordaens's majestic *Allegory of Fertility* has allowed us to bring to light things that were previously unknown.

To begin with, the analyses of the relining in "Automatic Thread Counting Analysis of Jordaens's Allegory of Fertility" conducted by Don H. Johnson (Rice University, Houston, Texas), C. Richard Johnson Jr. (Cornell University, Ithaca, New York), and Robert G. Erdmann (University of Arizona, Tuscon) in combination with information on provenance in the museum files has determined the period during which the latter was fabricated: the 18th century. In the wake of this discovery, our observations on the attachment of the lining canvas to the stretcher has allowed us to confirm the period in which the latter was made: the mid-18th century. This is nothing short of an extraordinary date for a stretcher frame with keys – extraordinary because it is so rarely found in the collections of the world's museums.

Concerning the pictorial layer, if certain chemical reactions have become visible to the eye, such as repainting, underdrawing, or the alteration of certain pigments, there is also another phenomenon to be observed: saponification. We are moreover the first to register its appearance, as it has never been recorded in reports of previous restorations carried out by restorers working for the museum. The article by Silvia A. Centeno and Dorothy Mahon, "The Chemistry of Aging in Oil Paintings: Metal Soap and Visual Changes" (*Metropolitan Museum Journal* 40, 2005, pp. 12–19) offers us a great deal of information that is important not only for the restoration but also for the conservation and understanding of artworks.

Finally, one may point to an anecdote concerning an outdated technique: the production of artificial craquelure. In effect, we have discovered the presence of artificial craquelure in one of the lacunae (the largest), located on the elbow of the crouching satyr. We must take into account that at the time, the old character of the work was considered of primary importance. Today, it is the work's authenticity that is foregrounded, for this constitutes its most important aspect.

Thread Count Analysis of Jordaens's *Allegory of Fertility*

DON H. JOHNSON

Radiographs of the Brussels *Allegory of Fertility* were subjected to thread-count analysis using a computer-based algorithm described elsewhere.[1] Briefly, the thread counting software estimates the thread densities of the horizontal and vertical threads over 1.25 × 1.25 cm squares on a 0.5 cm grid. In addition to the thread count, the thread angles (departures from horizontal and vertical) are also measured, which provides information about cusping. With this information, we can gain insights into how the canvas was prepared. As is often the case with Jordaens's work, the overall canvas consists of smaller canvas sections that have been sewn together. By examining thread density variations, we can infer which sections, if any, came from the same canvas roll. The cusping information reveals the locations of the strainer attachment points when the canvas was prepared. Consequently, we can determine which parts of the canvas were prepared together and which were prepared individually before being attached to other canvas sections. While the attachment point spacing on opposite sides could differ, the cusping depths and strengths should be similar unless an edge has been cut down after preparation. In this case, weaker and shallower cusping would indicate the cut-down side and allow an estimate of how much canvas was removed.

Figure 1 shows a composite radiograph of the painting. Each radiograph was scanned at 500 dpi at 8-bit resolution. Despite incomplete coverage of the painting, the radiographs provide insight into the three component canvases that were used to create the support. The main canvas, labeled A in figure 67, consists of two canvases sewn together with a vertical seam. Narrow canvas segments B and C were sewn to canvas A along the bottom, and the top and right edges, respectively.

Individual radiographs were subjected to automatic thread-count analysis, the results of which are shown in figure 68. Seams joining the component canvases can be seen after close inspection of the radiograph and are more clearly delineated by the thread-count results. The horizontal thread count results clearly indicate the location of the vertical seam in the central canvas. The average thread counts for the

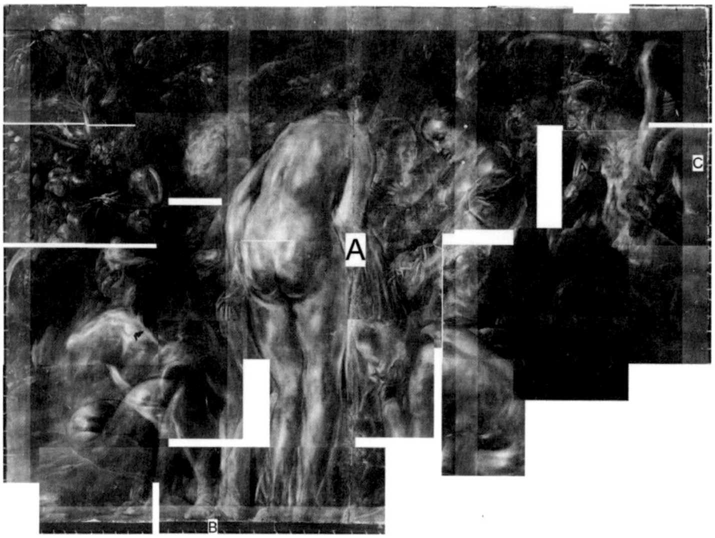

67. Composite radiograph of *Allegory of Fertility*. A composite radiograph was created from 44 individual radiographs. Coverage was incomplete but conclusions about the canvas support from thread counting were not affected.

various canvases comprising the painting's support are shown in table 1.

The main canvas is sufficiently large to determine warp/weft direction from the thread count results: vertical in the painting corresponds to warp threads. In addition, note that the variations in vertical-thread density have mirror symmetry about the vertical seam. We interpret this observation to mean that the two sections came from the same roll of canvas. One scenario that could explain this symmetry has the original canvas roll lain on the floor and then folded in half lengthwise, the length corresponding to the warp-thread direction. The canvas was then cut along the fold and the top portion flipped over to lie beside the bottom portion, maintaining the same orientation for the warp threads. The adjacent edges of the two canvas sections were then sewn together to create the main canvas.[2] The "flipping" results in mirror symmetry of the vertical-thread density variations.

The thread angles, shown in figure 69, reveal more about the construction of the painting's support. The large, repetitive angle changes that alternate between red and blue along the right edges correspond to cusping.

Note that the depth of cusping along the right edge extends further into the support than on the left. Judging by the depth of cusping, it appears that some 10 cm of canvas was removed from the painting's left side. Assuming that no canvas was removed from the right side as well, we can use the width of the right section to infer the width of the original canvas roll: about 120 cm, which corresponds to "7/4" ell.

Note that cusping can be seen along the bottom edges of canvas A and canvas B. Moreover, the cusping spacing differs for these canvases. It appears that canvas B was added to the bottom of canvas A after the main canvas was prepared, with canvas B primed separately. The presence of cusping in canvas B indicates that canvas B was not prepared before being attached to the larger canvas. Re-stretching the enlarged canvas and preparing the additions would be consistent with the cusping results. Canvas C was not sufficiently wide to visualize its cusping.

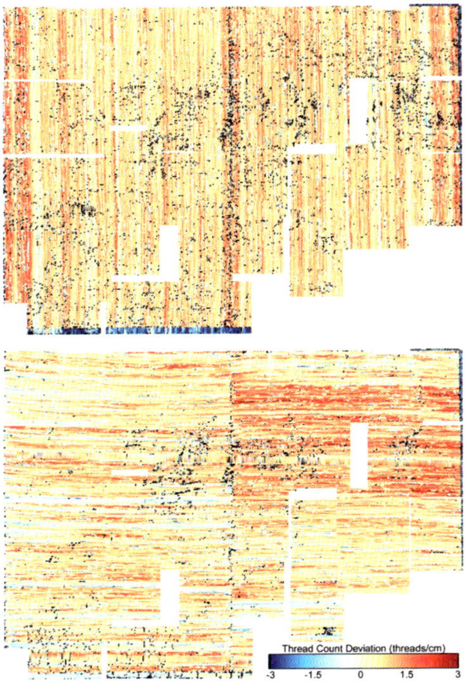

68. Thread density maps for vertical (top) and horizontal threads Thread density is indicated by a color displays the deviation of the thread count from the painting's average values: 13.2 threads/cm horizontal, 13.4 threads vertical. The relationship between color and thread-count deviation is shown in the color bar at the bottom. Black dots indicate locations where no measurement could be made.

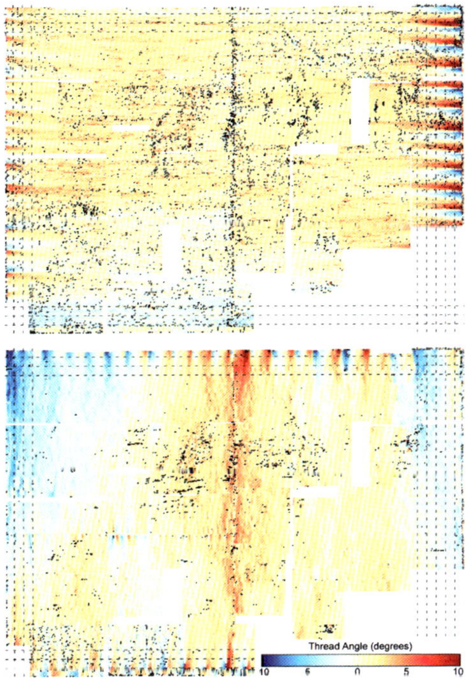

69. Thread angle maps for the vertical (top) and horizontal threads. The color bar shows how to translate color to angle. Positive angle (a redder color) corresponds to a counter-clockwise rotation of the threads, negative angle (a bluer color) to clockwise rotation. The gridlines along the edges allow measurement of the depth of cusping. They are 5 cm apart, with the line nearest the edge 5 cm from the radiograph's edge.

CANVAS	HORIZONTAL-THREAD COUNT	VERTICAL-THREAD COUNT
A	13.6 (0.8)	13.9 (0.7)
B	12.6 (0.6)	11.1 (1.1)
C	10.8 (0.8)	10.3 (0.8)

Table 1. Average thread-count results for each identified canvas. Canvas labels are shown in Figure 1. Thread counts (thread density measurements) are shown in threads/cm, with the standard deviation of the measurements shown in parentheses. The larger the standard deviation, the more the thread density varies.

[1] See Johnson et al. 2013 and Hendriks et al. 2013.

[2] This model for preparing a large canvas wider than the roll's width was suggested by Michiel Franken (Netherlands Institute of Art History, The Hague).

Appendix

Selected Bibliography

Antwerp 1993
R.-A. d'Hulst *et al.*, *Jacob Jordaens (1593–1678),* volume I: *Paintings and Tapestries,* Volume II: *Drawings and Prints,* exhibition catalogue, Antwerp, Koninklijk Museum voor Schone Kunsten. Brussels, 1993.

Bellini and Gritsay 2007
Rolando Bellini and Natalya Gritsay, *Rubens's Ceres: Two Original Versions,* exhibition catalogue, Saint Petersburg, State Hermitage Museum. Milan, 2007.

Brussels/Kassel 2012
Joost Vander Auwera, Irene Schaudies, and Justus Lange, *Jordaens and the Antique*, exhibition catalogue, Brussels, Royal Museums of Fine Arts of Belgium; Kassel, Museumslandschaft Hessen Kassel. Brussels, 2012.

Buschmann 1905
Paul Buschmann Jr, *Jacob Jordaens: Eene studie naar aanleiding van de tentoonstelling zijner werken ingericht te Antwerpen in MCMV.* Brussels, 1905.

Copenhagen 2008
Jorgen Wadum, Eva de la Fuente Pedersen *et al.*, *Jordaens: The Making of a Masterpiece*, exhibition catalogue, Copenhagen, Statens Museum for Kunst. Copenhagen 2008.

D'Hulst 1952
R.-A. d'Hulst, "Jacob Jordaens en de 'Allegorie van de vruchtbaarheid'", *Bulletin Musées royaux des Beaux-Arts / Bulletin Koninklijke Musea voor Schone Kunsten* 1 (March 1952), pp. 18–31.

D'Hulst 1974
R.-A. d'Hulst, *Jordaens Drawings,* 4 volumes. London, 1974.

Génard 1852
P. Genard, "Notice sur Jacques Jordaens", *Messager des Sciences historiques des arts et de la bibliographie de Belgique*, 1852.

Gritsay and Babina 2007
Natalya Gritsay and Natalya Babina, *State Hermitage Museum Catalogue: Seventeenth- and Eighteenth-Century Painting.* Saint Petersburg and New Haven, 2007.

Hendriks *et al.* 2013
Ella Hendriks, C. Richard Johnson, Jr, Don H. Johnson, Muriel Geldof, "Automated thread counting and the Studio Practice Project", chapter 9 in *Van Gogh's Studio Practice,* edited by Vellekoop *et al.*, pp. 156–81. Mercatorfonds, 2013.

Ingamells 1992
J. Ingamells, *The Dutch and Flemish Schools.* London, 1992.

Johnson *et al.* 2013
Don H. Johnson, C. Richard Johnson, Jr, Ella Hendriks, "Automated thread counting", chapter 8 in *Van Gogh's Studio Practice,* Edited by Vellekoop *et al.*, pp. 142–55, Mercatorfonds, 2013.

Koslow 1995
Susan Koslow, *Frans Snyders: Peintre animalier et de natures mortes*, 1597-1657. Antwerp, 1995.

Laureyssens 1993
Willy Laureyssens. *Jacob Jordaens in de Koninklijke Musea voor Schone Kunsten van België / Jacob Jordaens aux Musées Royaux des Beaux-Arts de Belgique.* Brussels, 1993.

Muller 1982
Jeffrey M. Muller, "Rubens' Theory and Practice of the Imitation of Art", *The Art Bulletin* 64 (1982), pp. 229–47.

Münch/Pataki 2012
Birgit Ulrike Münch and Zita Ágota Pataki, eds., *Jordaens: Genius of Grand Scale – Genie grossen Formats,* Cultural and Interdisciplinary Studies in Art, 10. Trier, 2012.

Paris 2013
Alexis Merle du Bourg, ed., *Jordaens 1593–1678,* exhibition catalogue, Paris, Petit Palais. Paris, 2013.

Peeters 2007
Natasja Peeters, ed., *Invisible hands? The Role and Status of the Painter's Journeyman in the Low Countries ca. 1450–ca. 1650,* Groninger Studies in Cultural Change, 23, edited by M. Gosman. Leuven-Paris-Dudly, MA, 2007.

Robels 1989
Hella Robels, *Frans Snyders: Stilleben- und Tiermaler, 1579-1657.* Munich, 1989.

Rooses 1906
Max Rooses, *Jacob Jordaens.* Antwerp 1906.

Rubinstein 1976
Ruth Olitsky Rubinstein, "A bacchic sarcophagus in the Renaissance", *The Classical Tradition.* British Museum Yearbook, 1, pp. 103–56.

Vander Auwera 2003
Joost Vander Auwera, "Leven, milieu en oeuvre van Abraham Janssen van Nuyssen (ca. 1571/75 –Antwerpen 1632), 'een seer fameus meester ende schilder in synen levene'. Een bijdrage tot de studie van de historieschilderkunst in de Zuidelijke Nederlanden tijdens de eerste helft van de zeventiende eeuw." PhD dissertation, Rijksuniversiteit Gent, 2003.

Vander Auwera 2007
Joost Vander Auwera, "Rubens and his Visual Sources: 'Just as the bee imbibes from several of the most beautiful flowers in order to incorporate nectar into its own honey'", *Rubens: A Genius at Work,* pp. 66–70, exhibition catalogue, Brussels, Royal Museums of Fine Arts of Belgium. Brussels, 2007.

Van der Meulen 1994
Marjon Van der Meulen, *Rubens Copies after the Antique,* Corpus Rubenianum Ludwig Burchard XXIII, 3 volumes. London, 1994.

Van Kalck *et al.* 2003
Michèle Van Kalck, ed., with the cooperation of Ingrid Goddeeris and Virginie Devillez. *De Koninklijke Musea voor Schone Kunsten van België: Twee eeuwen geschiedenis.* Brussels-Tielt, 2003.

Photo credits

Alinari Archives, Reproduced with permission of Ministero per i Beni e le Attività Culturali: p. 60, fig. 32

© Archivio dell'Arte - Luciano Pedicini / fotografo, p. 59, fig. 28

Bass Museum of Art, Gift of John and Johanna Bass: p. 22, fig. 1

bpk-images / Bildagentur für Kunst, Kultur und Geschichte / Bayerische Staatsgemäldesammlungen München: p. 24, fig. 4

bpk-images / Bildagentur für Kunst, Kultur und Geschichte / Sammlung des Regierenden Fürsten von Liechtenstein: p. 25, fig. 5

Bremen, Kunstsammlungen Böttscherstrasse, Museum im Roselius-Haus: p. 36, fig. 13

By kind permission of the Trustees of the Wallace Collection: p. 12–17, fig. 2; p. 53, fig. 35a and 35b; p. 74, fig. 35; p.81

Courtesy Bruno Mottin: p. 55, fig. 24

Dresden, Gemäldegalerie Alte meister, Staatliche Kunstsammlungen: p. 30, fig. 11; p. 49, fig. 19

Freya Maes: pp. 84–92

KIK /IRPA: p. 60, fig. 31 and 31a

Lukas- Art in Flanders vzw, photo: Hugo Maertens: p. 55, fig. 25

Lucerne, collectoin Hermann Alexander Beyeler: p. 28, fig. 9

Madrid Museo del Pardo: p. 26, fig. 6

Moscow, Pushkin State Museum of Fine Arts / Giraudon / The Bridgeman Art Library: p. 23, fig. 2

Museu do Caramulo, Fundação Abel e João de Lacerda: p. 23, fig. 3

Photo (C) RMN-Grand Palais (Musée du Louvre) © Hervé Lewandowski: p. 59, fig. 29

Photo (C) RMN-Grand Palais (musée du Louvre) © René-Gabriel Ojéda: p. 54, fig. 23

Prof. Don H. Johnson (Rice University Texas): p. 97

RMFAB / J. Geleyns / roscan: p. 2; p. 6–11, p. 31, fig. 12; p. 38, fig. 14; p. 41, fig. 16; p. 51, detail; p. 52, fig. 20 + detail, fig. 21 + detail; p. 54, fig. 22; p. 56 + detail; p. 57, fig. 27; p. 58 detail 27a

SMK Photo, National Gallery of Denmark, Copenhague: p. 28, fig. 10; p. 39, fig. 15

The Trustees of the British Museum. All rights reserved: p. 26, fig. 7; p. 57, fig. 26; p. 58 detail 26a; p. 59 detail 26b; p. 59 fig. 30

Vienna, Kunsthistorisches Museum: p. 27, fig. 8

Royal Museums
of Fine Arts of Belgium

Royal Museums of Fine Arts of Belgium
www.fine-arts-museum.be
Rue du Musée 9
B-1000 Brussels
Tel.: + 32 (0)2 508 32 09
info@fine-arts-museum.be

General Director
Michel Draguet

Concept and Scientific Direction
Joost Vander Auwera and Irene Schaudies

Publication Service
Laurent Germeau

Editing
Irene Schaudies

Silvana Editoriale

Direction
Dario Cimorelli

Art Director
Giacomo Merli

Editorial Coordinator
Sergio Di Stefano

Copy Editor
Lorena Ansani

Layout
Nicola Cazzulo

Production Coordinator
Antonio Micelli

Editorial Assistant
Ondina Granato

Photo Editor
Alessandra Olivari, Silvia Sala

Press Office
Lidia Masolini, press@silvanaeditoriale.it

Silvana Editoriale S.p.A.
via dei Lavoratori, 78
20092 Cinisello Balsamo, Milano
tel. 02 453 951 01
fax 02 453 951 51
www.silvanaeditoriale.it

Reproductions, printing and binding
in Italy
Printed by Grafiche Antiga, Crocetta di Montello (TV)
May 2016